Humorous Cryptograms

Helen Nash &
Dorothy Masterson

STERLING

New York / London
www.sterlingpublishing.com

For Lena Bobrow, Emanuel Tov, and Audrey Gabrielli

STERLING and the distinctive Sterling logo are registered trademarks of Sterling Publishing Co., Inc.

Library of Congress Cataloging-in-Publication Data

Humorous cryptograms / [compiled] by Helen Nash and
    Dorothy Masterson.
        p.   cm.
     Includes index.
     ISBN 0-8069-3982-6
     1. Cryptograms.   2. Wit and humor.   I. Nash, Helen.
  II. Masterson, Dorothy.
  GV1507.C8H96   1995
  793.73—dc20   95-12624
                                                          CIP

20   19

Published by Sterling Publishing Company, Inc.
387 Park Avenue South, New York, N.Y. 10016
© 1995 by Helen Nash
Distributed in Canada by Sterling Publishing
^c/o Canadian Manda Group, 165 Dufferin Street
Toronto, Ontario, Canada M6K 3H6
Distributed in the United Kingdom by GMC Distribution Services
Castle Place, 166 High Street, Lewes, East Sussex, England BN7 1XU
Distributed in Australia by Capricorn Link (Australia) Pty Ltd.
P.O.Box 704, Windsor, NSW 2756, Australia

Sterling ISBN 978-0-8069-3982-7

Contents

Introduction

It's always a joy to find kindred spirits. The idea of *Challenging Cryptograms* was to provide a collection of puzzles that could be challenging but not frustrating; hence the optional clue offerings. I've received letters from puzzlers who completed the book with no clue help, as well as from others who wanted only an occasional assist. To my delight, they all reported fun doing the cryptograms. And so *Humorous Cryptograms* continues in the same format.

Instead of dedicating this book to my mother, I put her to work. At seventy, she espouses the belief that cryptograms are good brain exercise. She also believes that humor is a vital part of maintaining health. Since she's also my best friend, I want to do my part to keep her mentally alert to read the road maps on our frequent wanderings and to keep her laughing as we lose our way, which we usually do.

This collection is like our searches for the wetlands and wild things. The clues, tucked away in the middle of the book, are the road map. They're there after wrong turns and mistakes have exhausted our laughter at ourselves, or if we don't have the time or inclination to wing it alone. They're there to bring us home smiling.

The quotes in *Humorous Cryptograms* were chosen to provoke a smile or chuckle, to brighten a moment in your day. Maybe cryptograms are but an indulgence for idle moments. Maybe cryptograms are really aerobic activities for our brains and hearts and souls. Whatever, they are definitely fun, so enjoy yourself!   —*Helen Nash*

My daughter is a better driver than she admits, but she can't tell the difference between a herd of heron and a gaggle of geese.   —*Dorothy Masterson*

How to Use This Book

This book is organized into five sections:

1. The cryptograms: Witty or humorous quotations, along with their authors' names, author and book, or character and television program. These have been converted into puzzles, with each letter of the alphabet standing for another. Although each quote has its own code, within that quote the same letter will represent its corresponding letter throughout.

2. Clue One: A separate section atthe end of the cryptogram collection in which one clue, or letter equivalent, is offered for each puzzle.Since each puzzle has its own code, each puzzle will have a different clue offering. Clue One gives the brain a start, but it won't make the puzzle too easy to solve.

3. Clue Two: A separate section following the Clue One section, in which a second letter equivalent is given for each puzzle. Clue Two offers a hint that alone, or with the first clue, will lead towards the solution.

4. Solutions: The decoded quotations for each puzzle.

5. Index of Authors and Quotations.

Hints for Solving Cryptograms

1. Single-letter words will be "I" or "a."

2. Frequent use of the same three-letter word may indicate the word "the." Notice that the word "he" is part of the word "the."

3. An apostrophe is usually followed by "t" as in contractions (don't) or by "s" as in possessives (dog's tail). Remember that a word ending with a apostrophe is probably a plural noun ending in "s." An apostrophe at the beginning of a word indicates the initial letters have been dropped, like the "th" in the word "them."

4. A question mark at the end of a quotation tells you the first word is likely "who," "what," "when," "where," "how," or "why."

5. Certain consonants occur together, such as "th," "wh," "sh," and "ch."

6. Likewise, the position of letters at the end of a word may indicate common endings such as "-tion,""-ent,"or "-ant," "-ing," or "-ed."

7. Short, single-syllable words that have "-ed" or "-ing" added to them double their final consonant, such as in "beginning" or "hopped."

8. In a two-letter word, one letter must be a vowel.

9. Often the author's name can be figured out, thereby leading to more clues within the quotation itself.

10. If you reach an impasse, read the puzzle and let your mind fill in the blanks. The English language is based upon the basic structure of who is doing what, with descriptive or qualifying phrases rounding out the picture.

Cryptograms

1. C'SP ISPJ-PEWOGKPE ARNPYT CH. *(I've over educated myself in)*
GYY KVP KVCHDN C NVIWYEH'K VGSP *(all the things I shouldn't have)*
BHIQH GK GYY. —HIPY OIQGJE *(known at all. —Noel Coward)*

2. M XIIZ HTUSLKLJ TU KIS UIDLIKL NCI *(A good listener is not someone who)*
CMU KISCTKX SI UMQ. M XIIZ HTUSLKLJ *(has nothing to say. A good listener)*
TU M XIIZ SMHELJ NTSC M UIJL SCJIMS. *(is a good talker with a sore throat)*
—EMSCLJTKL NCTSLCIJK *(—Katherine Whitehorn)*

3. QGM USF'L LWSUZ SF GDV VGYES *(You can't teach an old dogma)*
FWO LJAUCK. —VGJGLZQ HSJCWJ *(new tricks. —Dorothy Parker)*

4. PFL TRE JRP NYRK PFL CZBV RSFLK *(You can say what you like about)*
CFEX UIVJJVJ, SLK KYVP TFMVI R *(long dresses but they cover a)*
DLCKZKLUV FW JYZEJ. —DRV NVJK *(multitude of shins. —Mae West)*

5. YA FXM RLHC CX ZTC PYG XA *(If you want to get rid of)*
KCYHSYHZ XGXPK YH CJT SYCOJTH, *(stinking odors in the kitchen,)*
KCXB OXXSYHZ. —TPNL QXNQTOS *(stop cooking. —Erma Bombeck)*

6. BNMETRHNM HR Z VNQC VD GZUD *(Confusion is a word we have)*
HMUDMSDC ENQ ZM NQCDQ VGHBG HR *(invented for an order which is)*
MNS TMCDQRSNNC. —GDMQX LHKKDQ *(not understood. —Henry Kimmer)*

7

7. ZYRFC RUGAC Y BYW RM ZC
PCYJJW AJCYL, MLAC Y BYW RM ZC
NYQQYZJW AJCYL, MLAC Y UCCI RM
YTMGB ZCGLE Y NSZJGA KCLYAC.

—YLRFMLW ZSPECQQ

8. KYTHT ZJ UN JCVY KYZUM QJ
VNUBTHJQKZNU. ZK ZJ QU ZEECJZNU.
KYTHT QHT ZUKTHJTVKZUM
GNUNENMCTJ, KYQK ZJ QEE.

—HTITVVQ LTJK

9. TQ JZF LCP QZZWTDS PYZFRS EZ MP
NZYEPYEPO, OZY'E DSZH TE, MFE
RCFXMWP HTES ESP CPDE.

—UPCZXP V. UPCZXP

10. ZCXBCGC FC, RHJ AEGC SH YCS JT
CEUXR BO RHJ MEVS SH YCS HJS HO
ZCW.   —YUHJDAH FEUK

11. CQOWUP QJ BWXQHO AHS BMJCWHK
VAA UWHP. UAHAOWUP QJ VBS JWUS.

—SGQNW ZAHO

12. XRTKLV VOFTL HL. K EDY'W PFYW
WD URW HQ BFWL KY WML MFYEV DB
WPLINL ULDUIL PMD PLTLY'W LNLY
VHFTW LYDRAM WD ALW DRW DB XRTQ
ERWQ.   —HDYKOF UKULT

13. RXFKQ WA FJMR XLH RXFKQ WA URH
BXCRM X BXKR GRXKWGQ XLH
DRXKWGQ XLH HRXH.

                         —ZXBRM WGEFURF

14. YK X IFA ELNOT FMZF VFLJ DXO, YZ
YT WGSXLTG QG YT KFMI FK VFL; WLZ
YK X SXZ IFGT ZQG TXNG ZQYMA, YZ YT
WGSXLTG VFLJ DXO YT PXJNGJ.

                         —X.M. PQYZGQGXI

15. U LILVYUBRQL GF OYGNNIB BVN NV
GBSVYL NXI YIURIY TQN NV AYVNIHN
NXI OYGNIY.   —RIUB UHXIFVB

16. G NKM'E OYFZ SKFZH—G SPHE
JYEUA EAZ WKQZBMOZME YMN BZIKBE
EAZ TYUEH.   —JGDD BKWZBH

17. LG VQZMWIQ-JF-SXA AQZMI XF
YFYHYXS LYQEIQ HMZQG. MWI PJDMJL
RZM BJSSIE VG X LXF CQZL XFZMWIQ
VZZB.   —QZVIQM HGSPIHMIQ

18. Y SHYJOSQ EYJH YTAJO ZDMH
XDKBAEHB HYXS QHYM DKH YKT Y SYJR
OGEHB SGB DVK VHGISO GK DOSHM
LHDLJH'B LYOGHKXH.

                        —PDSK ALTGFH

19. YR DRHSKKSAHJYK DB Y CYR UFE
WESBR'H XREU FEU HE MYLX Y IDXS.

                    —BMDLE H. YNRSU

20. VNQQDPV UCXXDNB DF C MEQ MDYN
VNQQDPV DPQE C QRA EW OEQ KCQNX.
CWQNX JER VNQ RFNB QE DQ, DQ
CDP'Q FE OEQ.   —UDPPDN SNCXM

21. AV KFSEZAGXUNF PSM S DNFV
XGIKU PGASE. MUN CIFLNZ XUFNN
UIMCSEZM. XPG GB XUNA PNFN OIMX
ESTTLEK.   —FLXS FIZENF

10

22. NZD LTN UV XUP PDEHXGLNHUG
UG LBB HGEIWLGTD CUBHTHDE; KZHTZ
JDLGE, WUIXZBA, NZLN AUI TLGGUN YD
HGEIWDP VUW NZD LTTHPDGNE NZLN
LWD JUEN BHRDBA NU ZLCCDG NU AUI
                    —LBLG TUWDG

23. KV K CEW QX JKAD E WDVKTKQKXT
XV IEYKQEZKUB, K NXHZW UEP: QCD
YMXIDUU NCDMDRP EBDMKIET JKMZU
QHMT KTQX EBDMKIET NXBDT.
                    —ICMKUQXYCDM CEBYQXT

24. MEVPFZFXKP QEFKH QEBV AL X ILQ
CLO X MXQFBKQ TEBK QEBV DFSB EFP
AFPBXPB X KXJB.
                    —FJJXKRBI HXKQ

25. LPBUVEMVS TQZTFJFQFPT
PWPVFJUC ZS FAP JCVUBDPFPCF BMCS
YUE MDDUJCFBPCF ZS FAP VUEEQDF
YPR.
                    —KPUEKP ZPECMEL TAMR

26. IJ HVI DN MZNKJINDWGZ AJM CDN
AVOCZM. OCVO DN ZIODMZGT CDN
HJOCZM'N VAAVDM.

—HVMBVMZO OPMIWPGG

27. TZEXFY T CNGEXFY CGXBDG CWTB
WD BWXFEZ TKNOB LGXBXLZ XZ JXED
TZEXFY T JTRA-ANZB WNC XB PDDJZ
TKNOB VNYZ.

—LWGXZBNAWDG WTRABNF

28. IWPI NDJIWUJA HEPGZAT XC WXH
TNTH XH RPJHTS QN WXH RDCIPRI
ATCHTH, LWXRW WT ZTTEH WXVWAN
EDAXHWTS.　　　　—HWTXAPW VGPWPB

29. WJ ATLANP EO W IWJ SDK DWO IWZA
WHH PDA IEOPWGAO SDEYD YWJ XA
IWZA EJ W RANU JWNNKS BEAHZ.

—JEAHO XKDN

30. YLBMRY—ZYBR CK EJOLVIG BJL
BMZBKG IJOVDOVU RQ ALEQJL RYLK
EBMM IQZV.　　　　—WYKMMOG IOMMLJ

31. D'B T RAIPFWONH XANKFCFFZFW.
FLFWM UDBF D EFU PDLAWGFP, D CFFZ
UXF XANKF. —SKT SKT ETVAW

32. DROBO KBO DGY MVKCCOC SX QYYN
CYMSODI SX OXQVKXN. DRO
OAEOCDBSKX MVKCCOC KXN DRO
XOEBYDSM MVKCCOC.
—QOYBQO LOBXKBN CRKG

33. O NTA'M WXR MKHGTJCJR
OAZCAOMR CZ C HXJNKJ NKYKAZK.
WJKCUOAB OAMT ZTHKTAK'Z LTHK CAN
OJTAOAB CEE MLKOJ SETMLKZ OZ
MKHGTJCJR OAZCAOMR.
—ZXK UTEOAZUR

34. O WOQN RMA RMJAA DPLEJ
PNDOQOGRJPROZA KJEYVADG EQ P
XPDKHG PJA GAS WEJ RMA
GRHNAQRG, PRMVAROXG WEJ RMA
PVHDQO, PQN KPJCOQB WEJ RMA
WPXHVRT. —XVPJC CAJJ

35. QOBXEDGEL BOGJZ MXFODJBOJW
KL QVZENZZVXJ, KNW VW VZ XJAL
OCCOEWVFO VC LXN EGJ ZWXR ROXRAO
WGAIVJM.

—EAOBOJW GWWAOO

36. AQ ECEVGW IZE Z ESXCZJ
XSKEXCGKXG KSP. EIG EVCJJ PGZWE
IGW HDW XSZV, YDV ZXWSEE VIG
YZXB EIG'E GAYWSCUGWGU Z
EZAFJGW VIZV EZQE "WGEV CK
FGZXG"   —RDJCZ PCJJCE

37. QD QFFUQIUH YI EDU MXE VUUTI Q
SHESETYBU—XEFYDW JXQJ YJ MYBB
UQJ XYC BQIJ.   —MYDIJED SXKHSXYBB

38. CRY L BEOT'Y WLOOLTZ PSA. L
BEO BPLOVSALTZ LT PSA UQRYP.

—MPLMQ UEAF

39. BG UTBMBGZ T FHNLXMKTI PBMA
VAXXLX, TEPTRL EXTOX KHHF YHK MAX
FHNLX.   —A.A. FNGKH

14

40. R WLMTBYRA ASJFJ WRGF LF
ZBASLZD INA R SJRWQRLAJU QSB'F
RTTBQJW AB FLA WBQZ
BEERFLBZRTTG.　　—MJAJU NFALZBO

41. GURER NER GVZRF JURA
CNERAGUBBQ FRRZF ABGUVAT OHG
SRRQVAT GUR ZBHGU GUNG OVGRF LBH.
　　　　　　—CRGRE QR IEVRF

42. UXPR OUUA OYSPH EWWF AYDSYWH.
CDA OYSPH AUX'L NDQW LNW LYTW.
　　　　　　—LDPPIPDN CDXENWDA

43. FPXWA PXLAWVPWSAL WPX, YI
ZYVPLX, SYACKSF TVA NYVACTPYACXGL.
ACXPX KL SY JYKSA KS FYKSF AY ACXN
KI YSX KSAXSEL AY OXXJ YSX'L TXGA
TVZOGXE.
　　　　　　—IPXEXPKZ PWJCWXG

44. SHSNKTHD'U C HSNNTFZS
HGYRWGH. T JSCK, PGSNS'U TH
WYTKW HY SKO?　　　—HYJ UHYAACNO

15

45. RSPP, W CGDS LZS QLZVLPGHWLZ.
ZL QGZEWEGHS RGV SDSB SPSQHSE SJ-
XBSVWESZH KN VTQC G PGBUS
AGMLBWHN!   —RWPPWGA CLRGBE HGIH

46. Q CWSQF ZQBH DSJDTS MQUS
KJZS XD FJ ZS QBE QNASE MJV Y
ZQBQCS FJ CSF NJ ZXKM VJWA EJBS
QBE NFYTT ASSD TJJAYBC NJ
EYNNYDQFSE.   —WJGSWF GSBKMTSH

47. BUSQS VQS EWXH BNE SOEBAEWP
AW V DXVWS: MEQSJEO VWJ BSQQEQ.
                    —EQPEW NSXXSP

48. JGP GCDWPQJ BPCDQ KX IKEP CDP
JGHQP MPJFPPX JPX CXW QPUPXJB.
                    —GPIPX GCBPQ

49. E GFVGCVWEFGS RF W TCOEZEFA
VCEY VMWV IWZ ZR QOTM XOF VMWV E
MWS VR ZEFD QP PWTMV VR QWDG QP
AOGZVZ AR MRQG.
                    —X. ZTRVV XEVJAGCWHS

50. GMOU WMS TSBBJ-IQVNZW NEW
ZMOS KH KUS OIZGNAS; MK MO KUSMZ
VNJ HG GNBBMED.   —NEWZS DMWS

51. R'A LGNRUGH JXUGO OYC DUACZ'H
SRXCNJORUZRHOH. OYCB PCCI
TCOORZT GI UZ HUJIXUVCH JZM
INUQSJRARZT OYJO DUACZ JNC
XNRTYOCN OYJZ ACZ. OYJO'H ONGC,
XGO RO HYUGSM XC PCIO KCNB WGRCO
UN RO NGRZH OYC DYUSC NJQPCO.
                    —JZROJ SUUH

52. DB SKD QSZZ VU SUAZKUR, HBN
FPBNZR PKIS MTSKEOKFD DPTSS DVCSF
K RKH.
              —Q. FBCSTFSD CKNAPKC

53. U SQ OCSKF VZ QCCV QF QSLCO.
JICVICO QF QSLCO UH YOCYSOCK MZO
VIC ZOKCSW ZM QCCVUXA QC UH
SXZVICO QSVVCO.
              —JUXHVZX GIBOGIUWW

54. Z DFRWX XVMVWHKP
RJXRMRXOZWRUN WHJB CVYHSV FV
XVMVWHKP UZPUV. R FZMV PVVJ QN
IRXP PUSZBBWV RJUH UFV IRUDFVJ RJ
UFV QHSJRJB GRUF HOUYRUP UFZU
JVVX HJWN HJV ZDDVPPHSN: ZJ
VQKUN BRJ CHUUWV.   —VSQZ CHQCVDI

55. CFJUXMW FJU MZU TFWM CUDCTU
DX UFJMZ SZD DBLZM MD ZFGU
YZOTQJUX.   —WFIBUT EBMTUJ

56. BNHI BL BHCI PQ H QIGVK INHI
QIHVIQ BPIN HC LHVINTOHRL HCA
BGVRQ PIQ BHK OX IG H DEPSHU.
                          —QHSOLE WGEABKC

57. HDBMG YTTW DY GXT BTHJBZ JH
XJMNDGRI ZRYRETZTYG? GXRG'M TRMV!
GXT WTRGX JH RII
WDTGDGDRYM, RYW GXT
BTMOBBTPGDJY JH R HBTYPX PXTH.
                        —ZRBGDY X. HDMPXTB

58. SNP SWVLDOP UGSN YLIP IMYTGYQ
GB SNMS YVS PAPWCSNGYQ BSVJB
UNPY SNP ZLBGT BSVJB.

    —BGW WVDPWS NPOJZMYY

59. Q ATF'I RFTX CTX ZTW BOOE MYTWI
TEA MPO... YWI QF SZ NMVO, Q AQAF'I
OJOF VOO QI NTSQFP. QI CQI SO BHTS
ICO HOMH.

    —GCZEEQV AQEEOH

60. H VFRG YJ GFNVFZ H MTV OTZJ
VHZTG KETU H MF FU X GHTV, CF ET
MXOT YT BTB BHRRC. QUFK KEXV
EXBBTUTG? H XVT AXCVTZ.

    —DFT T. RTKHC

61. DAS VGGK DAEZV LPGXD VGEZV
DG QGXY DHSZDQ-CECDA AEVA
BUAGGN YSXZEGZ EB DALD QGX VSD DG
BSS LNN QGXY GNK UNLBBRLDSB. DAS
PLK DAEZV EB DALD DASQ VSD
DG BSS QGX.   —LZEDL RENZSY

62. S GNMUMG MF S TSD LCB ODBLF
UCZ LSP QVU GSD'U KNMXZ UCZ GSN.

—OZDDZUC UPDSD

63. S AHDHV EVYDHB NSERLME KO
TSYVO. LAH WRLMBT YBNYOW RYDH
WLKHERSAI WHAWYESLAYB EL VHYT
SA ERH EVYSA.   —LWUYV NSBTH

64. VWW RCNVGICNE ZIEG WNVCX GY
RYNOFEG. GSVG'E MSQ GSN TCYMX
TNVC VXP GSN LFNWP ZYIEN RVX
ESVCN GSNFC WFKNE VXP WFKN FX
SVCZYXQ. YL RYICEN, GSNQ RVX'G
ZVGN YC GSN ZFRN MYIWP NOUWYPN.

—TNGGQ MSFGN

65. W CWH YNQ NWZ HJFJI SQHJ VQ
ZENQQD CWM ZVJWD BIQC W BIJUSNV
EWI, GTV UB NJ NWZ W THUFJIZUVM
JLTEWVUQH, NJ CWM ZVJWD VNJ YNQDJ
IWUDIQWL.

—BIWHODUH L. IQQZJFJDV

20

66. HPIV BNOBKWBIYB XCL ACGVXA EB
AXCA WI BIVHCIF IPZPFU VPBL AP AXB
AXBCABK GIHBLL XB PK LXB XCL
ZKPIYXWAWL.   —RCEBL CVCAB

67. ZKDNBQ TDCC QBS TBKJ AQSDC TH
NSGKS NHQFDQP G WHSSHK OCGNN BE
ZHBZCH SIHKH. —CGAKHQOH X. ZHSHK

68. W PNGFQV'R ZWVQ OTWVE LKFFTQ
ZWQQFT-KETQ WC NVFD W BVTP K CTP
ZNHT NVT-XGVQHTQ-DTKH-NFQ
ATNAFT.   —QTKV ZKHRWV

69. F NYA AC OCJH NLFRFJH DW LVSFVN
RPYR F JVSVL HCR YLCMJZ RC LVYZFJH
RPV XCCE.   —HLCMTPC DYLU

70. HLID QUYQGU RYIOXTUA JZU
JZXIFO NZXRZ FYEUAIHUIJ TYUO PYA
JZUH JY SU OYRXLG QAYFAUOO, SCJ
JZUD RYIOXTUA JZU JZXIFO
FYEUAIHUIJ TYUO PYA YJZUAO LO
OYRXLGXOH.   —ULAG NLAAUI

71. UJD BCUD, R UJCFPJU, XDYZV
ZCUJRZP UC OCXDZ. OD VJCFTL WD
YIXDL.   —DLZY C'WIRDZ

72. MECZCRCU W QCCX XWYC
CPCUOWVC, W XWC LSMZ JZGWX GEC
QCCXWZT HNVVCV.
                    —USKCUG F. EJGOEWZV

73. WUJQ FOJS WM OUMMW OULAYJQ
WJVBYJ WUAMFKU KHFDJ. WUJQ MFKUW
WM OUMMW VJ WUAMFKU YLCMYJFV.
                    —WHYYFYHU RHCGUJHS

74. XDG HGKQ EZP EAEJQ QDVIUP QNX
PVKZ EZP QGXXUG XDGNA
PNOOGAGZBGQ UNSG LVVP
BDANQXNEZQ.   —QEWIGU LVUPKFZ

75. XW QXRUQT YCWJTM VSVP OJUE
JE WX ACV MRXRXI-PWWU KJPXRAJPV
JXTVYY QGYWTJAVTL FVPAQRX ACQA CV
FQX CWTM CRY WHX RX ACV
FWXSVPYQARWX.   —KPQX TVGWHRAD

76. KNPRLRY ZFGS, "GU'Z IPU
KNRUNRY CPH KGI PY QPZR UNFU
BPHIUZ," WYPDFDQC QPZU.

—XFYUGIF IFLYFUGQPLF

77. A IATG AX DNJK UZXAUIRATW XN SK
Z SZG BOZRKJ ZX WNOI. XEK
HNJUK RNY BOZR, XEK SKXXKJ RNY
JKDKDSKJ XEK NQQZUANTZO WNNG
UENX.   —TYSZJ WYOSKTMAZT

78. XZGLQ JWMJDWLCJZW JY JW XZYC
ULYAY CVZ BAGUAWC XZGLQ, OZGCP-
AJDSC BAGUAWC JWMJDWLCJZW, LWM
OJOCP BAGUAWC AWHP.

—HJCCZGJZ MA YJUL

79. JWZNZ XC AMJWXAI XA JWZ GMNFT
X GMQFTA'J TM EMN WMKZ, LAT
JWZNZ XC AMJWXAI WZ GMQFTA'J TM
EMN BZ.... GZ CKZAT MQN FXUZC TMXAI
AMJWXAI EMN ZLRW MJWZN.

—PXAI RNMCPS

80. ZFT IJTQHLV UJFUWJ, HZQJT
ZLZQA, WLQLKHQLFV QHMJD QYJ UWHIJ
FZ DJO.   —KFTJ PLSHW

81. RN IYC JSBL LY AY S LDRBQ
ESATI, IYC DSWM LY JYXZ SL RL SP
LDYCQD IYC JSBL LY AY RL JMTT.
                          —FMLMX CPLRBYW

82. WULBL SFK XH XLLV WH VH FXN
UHDKLSHBZ FW FCC. FTWLB WUL TGBKW
THDB NLFBK WUL VGBW VHLKX'W ILW
FXN SHBKL.
                          —ODLXWGX PBGKE

83. KUZCQAG CVFSKVZ TZ CKFC WVR
FRN RFCUQRZ PVKFEV MUZVXG QRSV
CKVG KFEV VLKFTZCVN FXX QCKVA
FXCVARFCUEVZ.   —FPPF VPFR

84. GEOKU KUZKU WK IGU SEEY
MQYSXUZI CGWNG BUUHK GEOKUK
DOEX AUIIWZS EZ HUEHFU.
                          —C.N. DWUFYK

85. T LVHI BA KH VYAF FETBH... KLB T
IXTCBHI.   —JQH FHVB

86. R GSVOQ QHEGK TRLW PSV LROO
LWK GSTZ GSYK WSYK. MKLLKA
ZLROO, R'OO QHEGK TRLW LWK GSTZ
HEQ PSV GSYK WSYK.

                    —FASVGWS YHAC

87. DJZK Q TEWZ CETO GY AFCMQK, Q
DER TYFSG-WESGQEMZA QK WP
ECRZKTZ EKA RZKGZKTZA GY AZEGJ QK
WP ECRZKTZ, RY Q REQA GJZP TYFMA
RJYYG WZ QK WP ECRZKTZ.

                    —CSZKAEK CZJEK

88. N JFY YTT RFSD YA INSSJWX. N'AJ
LTYYJS YT YMJ UTNSY BMJWJ JAJWD
YNRJ N XJJ FQZRNSZR KTNQ N XYFWY
YT XFQNAFYJ.   —JQQJS TWHMNI

89. LFQYWFC WFC WXLZBKW WZL JRH
KHVFJZBLG GLAWZWJLC ND JSL GWXL
YWFQVWQL.   —QLHZQL NLZFWZC GSWR

                    25

90. B PV UVH NKSR HV FDRKZ BCC VT
KUQ YKU IRWBUP WBF IKNZ, IMH B
IRCBRGR HWR LRUHCRYKU BF KU
KHHVSURQ.   —FKYMRC XVWUFVU

91. QYL IAOI K IAKQW YD KI, K LKEA
K AOP HUUQ O AUJJ-ZOKEUZ LAUQ K
LOE IAKZIG GUOZE YJP. K IZKUP KI
LAUQ K LOE DKDIG, HRI K OJLOGE FYI
EJUUXG.   —FZYRVAY SOZM

92. L RWUK DYKCO W MZO ZE OLIK
DKWVJRLCB ORVZABR ORK SLSMK EZV
MZZYRZMKD.   —X.J. ELKMND

93. QOP YU NTK GPDA OPYQOD NTON
DKOZPU LA LKYPX TAJGSZYNYSOD. TK
JZKNKPRU NG LK JGDYNK OPR NTKP,
KMKPNVODDA, TK LKSGQKU JGDYNK.
                        —FKOP HKZZ

94. J HEXWNBM JY YKNIJYT, SKL J
QEM LW MNWZ JL SBDEKIB J NEY WKL
WO HJVA.   —XKMU LBYKLE

95. S JWHMIA! LXG CEMGCB-AWDWH
BWSGA M'DW OGSRCMRWK LXIGCWWH
EXIGA S KSB, SHK HXF CEWB RSQQ
YW S JWHMIA!   —OSPQX ASGSASCW

96. K BMA'H SNLP N XSMHMFCNXS, DQH
JMQ ONA SNLP ZJ UMMHXCKAHV. HSPJ
NCP QXVHNKCV KA ZJ VMOIV.
                    —FCMQOSM ZNCE

97. RC ZUX'IP CRCMZ ZPNIW UFB,
ZUX'LP HIUANAFZ UYGPB WU TNGZ
ONIW ZUX ONG'M PLPG IPTPTAPI NFF
UC MDPT RG UIBPI.   —NGBZ IUUGPZ

98. H QNJNYMTV KNJRFN R
JLQHBMHRY BJHNYMHBM. HM DRB MLN
EYTV LNRTML WTRY H JECTI RZZEQI.
                    —KNMBV BRTGHYI

99. E VHQY JTOY FT PYBHPC FVY UHG
JTSPFR XTF HR H JHFVYCPHU ASF
PHFVYP HR H JHREXT.
                    —PEJVHPC EXBPHOR

27

100. BESMUS MKKSBF TC
WSUHQDMFHPD. H YPD'F GMDF FP
RSEPDQ FP MDC KEOR FZMF GHEE
MKKSBF TS MU M TSTRSW.

—QWPOKZP TMWL

101. NVT ZNHVWVE W UXNR KV
TFTAXKVR WV ZD AKYKZKU. XNP XT ENR
WVRN ZD AKYKZKU W'FF VTJTH BVNP.

—EHNGLXN ZKHM

102. ZGZHI OHTS ACBBLB ZFP IVEQGL,
ICB SZQF GHTPVAI TO ICB ATVFIHW
QL ZPKTAZZI, Z PHQFR SZPB OHTS
EZUWBHL.   —ZEZF ATHBF

103. NKX PGR USC KN NTNPH, TP TM
SFESHM PGTXW SCW FKCB HSXWSBR,
ETPG S CRSXMTBGPRW DZSXPRXLSVQ.

—LTFF VKMLH

104. KAP CZKPOK OVYPDKYMYV
OKGSYPO OANX KAZK ZCC LYVP ZDS
FZKO AZJP VZDVPF.   —BGCYZ XYCCYO

28

105. DCJIXH LYTLNQ JCYA DX DN ALN
TLQ BCDFZS, EWJ F ZXGXH HXLYFPXA
JILJ F'A XZA WK EXFZS JIX QICHJXQJ
UZFSIJ CO JIX NXLH.

           —QFH SCHACZ HFBILHAQ

106. H WKKG XL RKC RPIPLLHSXEN
PLLPRCXHE QTLC OPIHTLP NKTS
IFXEG FHCPL XC.

           —YHCFPSXRP BFXCPFKSR

107. QYJTJ HTJ FVWA QBF QYLVKD H
IYLWS BLWW DYHTJ BLWWLVKWA—
IFGGCVLIHRWJ SLDJHDJD HVS YLD
GFQYJT'D HKJ.   —ST. RJVXHGLV DUFIM

108. Q GKW WEXZZE-WPKXE—DRE
RBYSXERBKEZIC EFZ WEXZZE GKW
XSNZS NXQJZ.   —HKXXQZ YQWFZX

109. QEADYJAA DA T QSMJ. D EAJ
CFTC AJNCDSY SH CFJ ZTZJM CS
WDYJ CFJ NTC QSK.   —AEJ VMTHCSY,
            "J" DA HSM JGDLJYNJ

110. NKX RJPXS NZC, OFSH ETPG PGR
VKFKX VKCPXKF ZCPTF T PZXC
BXRRC.   —WSYTW FRPPRXUSC

111. G BGUU AVQJAPYFQUC SDMF YJ
LFFH BSDY GL SDWWGUC HVJBV DL
ZDGVRAU FIWUJCIFVY, BSGES G DI
ZUDQ YJ LDC QJFL VJY QFLEXGPF
SJUQGVZ WAPUGE JRRGEF.
                      —QFDV DESFLJV

112. CFJ MJTWWO HMDVFCJYDYV CFDYV
TQSEC UDLLWJ TVJ DA CFJ XYSIWJLVJ
CFTC OSE'WW VMSI SEC
 SH DC.   —LSMDA LTO

113. FDXOFFAOQD AJ OU DWIDMMDUC
CDJC VY KPJC GVZ OXAIONMD BVPF
SAEVFID ZOJ.   —XOFQV TOPYXOU

114. CV JEYDA YWKBDUA QWGTAN CA
TWABA CUDP YGCAQ SBGC. ZJM U
QMUDD DUPA UM.   —"NAEEUQ MWA
                 CAEKYA," WKEP PAMYWKC

115. JV IC RGRYGFYS PGXYSQDC, YBJ
VGEF YSGVZL SDWWFVFQ: G QGQV'Y
YSGVH JVEF DPJAY PXJJHF LSGFUQL
DVQ G BDLV'Y YDHFV QGXFEYUC YJ
GVYFVLGMF EDXF.

                    —XDUWS LESJFVLYFGV

116. OCOGP VFY L VOOE ZFYEA ES
MGSEOBE VO. L BFY'E KLWHGO SHE
ZTFE KGSV.   —VFO ZOAE

117. OYZXLCT JEGC UJC JZUUCTU
WDTTCT. VCL-JCELT EVC HEDV-UZ-
QDLLYDXB UZVVDL, EXL OVFXCUUCT
EVC UJC HVDBDLCTU ZH EYY. DU'T
TZQCUJDXB UZ LZ RDUJ JZVQZXCT, XZ
LZFOU.   —VZXEYL VCEBEX

118. ROG QXWWGVGSNG IGRCGGS
QXPYVNG DSQ KGMDK HGFDVDRXYS XH
RODR D KGMDK HGFDVDRXYS MXPGH D
OLHIDSQ RXTG RY OXQG OXH TYSGE.
                    —AYOSSE NDVHYS

119. H BQZCWQT GU OZBD ZE Z YZYR,
ZWT H JZKQW'G JZT Z BQEEUW EHWVQ.
                         —XZCHBRW XUWCUQ

120. PARKHYRKP EDKU Y ZAAL IH RC
ODYZBTKU Y PIC HA RCPKZW,
"ZYZYIU, CAN PDANZB DIQK PHICKB I
QYTXYU."   —ZYZYIU OITHKT

121. XG ZBZGI, IEO CYEH GSXG BZ
MKMNIGSBYA PBP YEG GONY EOG XW
IEO SXP LTXYYMP, BG BW YEG GSM
ZXOTG EZ IEON LXNMYGW. GSMNM
XNM DXNCMG ZENQMW XG HENC.
                         —CXNMY PMQNEH

122. SY GVR LWAU W TOWXK SA UNK
FRA, GVR'MK CVU UV TRU RT LSUN W
YKL EOSFUKDF.
                         —WESCWSO MWA ERDKA

123. VDVIKOCLBU VWFV KEH UIEM EHO
EX, GHO KEH BVDVI IVQEDVI XIEZ
QCLWRCEER.   —GVIKW GNLBGILRUV

32

124. DWQ VROZN NWRERNDQEZODZNO
AL RPM SAAG ZPUQODZSRDAE REQ R
IXAGGZPS PRDJEQ RPG ZPLZPZDQ
IRDZQPNQ. OANZQDM WRO
ZPRGUQEDQPDXM VQQP SEAABZPS
TABQP DA DWZO QPG LAE MQREO.
　　　　—OJQ SERLDAP, "R" ZO LAE RXZVZ

125. ALMXRWUK LGTU KUTUW OUUK
TUWJ SYYR GV XMIVUKMKS VY VLUMW
UXRUWI, OEV VLUJ LGTU KUTUW
DGMXUR VY MHMVGVU VLUH.
　　　　　　　　—BGHUI OGXRNMK

126. VZB GOQL VZDOC KGWIB VZMO M
WBUGWFBT ADCMWBVVB IFGEBW DI MO
BMWQL AZWDIVFMI ZGXXBW.
　　　　　　　　—QDN IAGVV

127. GC JXNV GFKC GFS F
JFZDAHAICDV RXABS RCHMWC GAN
NVMJFIG QCDV AD HMW F IFWCCW MH
AVN MQD.　　　—JFWZFWCV GFBNCU

33

128. NDF TO ORSFMBTXD MBNM
HRFOX'M SNMMFZ, AXVFOO IRA NZF N
JBFFOF.   —LTVVTF LAZUF

129. BIP BO QG OJFPIKL UBZK QP LXP
SWL FI ZWHBJ OBJ UXFJUG-LFC
XBEJL. F KBI'U PTPI SWIU UB KB
WIGUXFIY UXWU OPPZL YBBK OBJ
UXFJUG-LFC XBEJL.   —JFUW JEKIPJ

130. A'K ONY KGVO MARYFWOYX HGKWL
AL ONY HGFMX. WLJ HGKWL ZWL RY
MARYFWOYX AI VNY HWLOV
OG RY. IAFVO, VNY NWV OG ZGLTALZY
NYF NSVRWLX.   —KWFONW KAOZNYMM

131. QB KMYKU QX HDJYKE, UVA FVRD
PV VPD UJX KUDQM UJQM LVPD QP J
TQHMJME?   —TQTE KVRTQP

132. XQ IC NYKSW HCSS YKO
CDTCOXCENCH QYO IAGL LACM NYHL
KH, IC'W VC PXSSXYEGXOCH.
                    —GVXRGXS FGE VKOCE

133. BK KJSMP J TXZJG KTMGKN
NMJVP KX ZJSM J ZJG XL DMV PXG,
JGO JGXKDMV TXZJG KTMGKN
ZBGIKMP KX ZJSM J LXXF XL DBZ.
                    —DMFMG VXTFJGO

134. MIH NVDYL UYJULHMH
VUICHFHNHJM YP MIH RYNHJ'E
NYFHNHJM YP MIH 1970'E RVE MIH
SZMUI MLHVM.   —JYLV HXILYJ

135. B QVSF FZ FTKK NZJ V FTAABRBY
EFZAN VLZJF ZAVK YZSFAVYTWFBZS.
B VECTG FDBE PBAK FZ EKTTW QBFD
HT VSG EDT EVBG SZ.   —QZZGN VKKTS

136. LVONO'X ZP WBUSO HZ U W.H.'X
BHMO MPN HQWULHOZSO,
MUHZLVOUNLORZOXX, PN
XBPWWHZOXX. H AZRONXLUZR LVO
XUQO YAUBHMHSULHPZX UWWBI MPN
VPAXOEHCOX.   —XAO JNUMLPZ,
                "T" HX MPN TANJBUN

137. GJY'P PCDA KX C TCY'H POTA
PCVDOYS CIJKP PMA HTCEPYAHH JZ
LJKE RMOVGEAY; MA UCYPH PJ PCVD PJ
LJK CIJKP PMA HTCEPYAHH JZ
MOH.   —A.U. MJUA

138. JX QXOEJ OEKKPMG RXK OXJMZ;
FNMZ EKM EAA TAMYMK MJXDCN,
SMRXKM OEKKZPJC E OPAAPXJEPKM, FX
REAA PJ AXYM QPFN NPO RPKGF.
                          —TMGEKM UEYMGM

139. FB'H ZODW TMD RY BM VYB IHYW
BM BZYHY XZOLVFLV BFRYH. F XOL
DYRYRAYD PZYL BZY OFD POH XUYOL
OLW BZY HYE POH WFDBJ.
                          —VYMDVY AIDLH

140. Q FSN S ZHJQPF NHCQBHKD: OFHD
YXERY DEL ELO JQOF OFH MQKPO
WSQX; OFHD JSYH DEL LW JFHX OFH
FSQKNKHPPHK PFEJP.
                          —ZESX KQBHKP

141. NX ... TFL WEH'D PY E KFFC
YUEVMZY, DBYH TFL'ZZ SLRD BEJY DF
PY E BFOONPZY IEOHNHK.

                      —WEDBYONHY ENOC

142. QTW LVC QTWLDH KRF "ARDDH RS
LVCWD ARS, MWPRYFW QTWH'DW ALDW
ARQYDW." MYQ QTW SWK QTWLDH OF:
"AWS CLS'Q ARQYDW. ARDDH R
HLYSUWD LSW."   —DOQR DYCSWD

143. T VJBNP'O CPGIP JPL GYNP
RJQQTJWNZ, OVGFWV UFTON J XNI
VJBN HNNP JAJQ.   —KZJ KZJ WJHGQ

144. RBAHGB UE DJB ZHC AJU
VGHLXBX AUZBC'X SLRBGHDLUC; JB
LX HRUMD DU OMLD JLX IUR.

                     —BGLTH IUCF

145. AC AE FASSANWXC CZ EII YGQ
XONI EGZWXF MI EZ IPUILEAKI. AC AE
HZECXQ GZXIE.

                —HOTQ YAXEZL XACCXI

146. T FKYNE ZPAMJZ NTJ KH AMJ
IKOP AMPH IFJJD RJHJPAM TA.

—IMTZNJV QKHZPH

147. ZQU XRG ZH QHCM R QADPRSM
ND ZH WUUB QNL R CNZZCU KURCHAD;
ZQU XRG ZH CHDU QNL ND ZH WUUB
QNL R CNZZCU LHIU KURCHAD.

—Q.C. LUSJWUS

148. QUW LWFPXANKRB FRLQH
KCPAYB'Q DREW PF QUWNL DNBYG
VUWQUWL N'Y XW DNGQREWB ZCL R
QLCAACF CL ZCL QUW SPWWB CZ
WBMARBY. XPQ GNAAH RG QUW
LWSPWGQ VRG, N GQCFFWY VWRLNBM
FPLFAW.   —WANJRXWQU QRHACL

149. WYFLOQ WYNTWOLK QIBGH HA
DIHQ QWIQ BUHQLZUZJ QA WUN UH
BUGL QOKUZJ QA OLIM TBIKFAK
NIJIPUZL RUQW KAYO RUDL QYOZUZJ
QWL TIJLH.   —FIOOK JABMRIQLO

38

150. NEQ WUPN AUAVYKD YKFUDPKIBXO
RQIBMQ NURKG BP PNBYY K EVPFKXR
LBNE WUXQG. —TUQG KRKWP

151. GRZMJA-DZOAZQM VYYVXVACN VXR
V TCXZWCN YJRQWBRQWQ—BVTJZQRN
ZQERQARS AW XRYDZTVAR AJR
UVTFUXRVFZQM BVQCVD DVUWX AJR
ZQSCNAXZVD XREWDCAZWQ XRDZRERS
CN WO. —NCR MXVOAWQ,
"R" ZN OWX REZSRQTR

152. VQRIFUJR OVTUB ED RVYQZJ BUYE
EVDXD DPDXCOVTUL TR—VD FRBR GD,
"XYRDFUUD, JY ED VFPD
FUC MVDDOYR ZDSO?" ZTBD VD MFU'O
LY YPDX OY OVFO RYSF MQRVTYU FUJ
ZTSO TO VTGRDZS. —XYRDFUUD IFXX

153. FDPR V FLH VR ULAJW, SDP
RGWHPH FJGUB UJJY LS KP LRB HLE,
"BJ EJG HSVUU SDVRY AUJRBPH DLQP
KJWP CGR?" —XJLR WVQPWH

154. WRVROWRONW VXT JOUT V
GOUOZO. CAVR RATH XTDTVJ OW
WPMMTWRODT, GPR CAVR RATH
NFZNTVJ OW DORVJ.

—VVXFZ JTDTZWRTOZ

155. O BDHM EYBM EXVHOME, DWH
ZMDAOXJ OE XUM AMDHOWF NDVEM YQ
EXZMEE DBYWFEX XUYEM OW XYVNU
ROXU OX.   —IDWM RDFWMZ

156. MI MQ UETA FUQQMNTB IU TMPB
WLFFMTA BPBS LVIBS UE L RLA-IU-
RLA NLQMQ.   —ZLSDLSBI NUEELEU

157. CUSTS EL LZ WECCWS
PEGGSTSOJS ISCFSSO URLIMOPL HZR
BENUC ML FSWW YSSA CUS GETLC.

—MPSWM TZNSTL LC. XZUO

158. GIXF I GIX CIW DIYYHX JX YBTH
MJRC I KJVY JX I YJKCR WB AJG CH
MBLYA XBR CITH SCBWHX I WLJR NF JR.

—GILVJSH SCHTIYJHV

40

159. PZG ULILA ALVXXP BUZK V WVU
GUEFX PZG'IL NFIZAQLN YFW.

                         —RCV RCV HVTZA

160. SEYCYAYH X OQUY Q FLJ, X
UEXCV, XM UEXM UEY TQC X SQCU TJ
ZEXIOHYC UR MDYCO UEYXH
SYYVYCOM SXUE?   —HXUQ HLOCYH

161. W VOHS RCWBU ZOIBRFM. W RCB'H
GSDOFOHS AM QCZCFG TFCA
AM KVWHSG. W DIH HVSA HCUSHVSF.
W ZSH HVSA ZSOFB TFCA HVSWF
QIZHIFOZ RWTTSFSBQSG.

                        —FWHO FIRBSF

162. JN ISSCI NB CS J IDSEN CT AJMS
JE VKG DBBAI, RLN TBL HEBU, NQKN'I
QBU J HSDN NGKVH BM UQKN UKI
OBJEO BE.   —RKGRKGK RLIQ

163. PM LZB TIR'H XIL IRLHYPRF FZZV
IQZBH XZSDZRD, XPH JPFYH YDJD QL
SD.   —INPTD JZZXDKDNH NZRFCZJHY

164. EW MTHXZGV ZGV N MZYS
RNQTFSV ITJ Z FSZCCW QIIV HWHJSE
ZXITJ JMS MITHSLIFA: GSNJMSF IGS
IR TH VISH NJ.   —VIJJNS ZFUMNXZCV

165. JSC NYC KSYZ JYMT ASBBSK
BEYC FRJSC. 'NYPTS RCGI BES JYGS
JXCZ NRPGZ NRCNSXUS RQ RCS XCNE
SLPYGXCH Y EPCZKSZ JXGST.
                    —KRTSYCCS YKCRGZ

166. NVYALSYAN S IVXFAP SM YAX
DXF IVYAX PADZZE NKSL ADJQ VLQAP.
TAPQDTN LQAE NQVKZF ZSBA XAGL
FVVP DXF UKNL BSNSL XVI DXF LQAX.
                    —WDLQDPSXA QATHKPX

167. OYGY OAZYW ZYVWI IA PA
YLYGSIMHWJ—OAGD VWP MVLY TVTHYN?
                    —RVWPHRY TYGJYW

168. OVLZ SWK'EL TZ WEIVWNWQ
OWEEFLE, GWYL NTSG TEL OWEGL IVTZ
WIVLEG.   —LEYT RWYRLPB

42

169. R ONFFPB RG WROS JUBNZ—AXJ
NW WUUG NW R DXGQ XH JDP HDUGP, R
CPFJ N FUJ APJJPI.

　　　—AXGGZ DUPWJ NGB EUDG IPRGPI

170. XMYE S XVK V DSLU S GEUO MVI
CXG TLSYEIK, VEI CMYO XYLY
SPVDSEVLO. VEI CMYO XGJUI GEUO
HUVO XSCM YVFM GCMYL.

　　　　　　—LSCV LJIEYL

171. VLMS WD JQUZ QGMS'U LQNND,
T'W SAU LQNND. SAU CMJQFZM T
JQGM QCAFU ULMTG WAAX, CFU
CMJQFZM T ISAV ULMD'GM PFZU
ZTUUTSE ULMGM ULTSITSE FN VQDZ
UA EMU MKMS.　　—NMSSD VQGX WAZMG

172. Q PNWZK S HNZY YESM ISQE NZ
BRAQZ'T DSXBRJ HSTJ ZQYIJ. QP QJ'T
SZNJIRE CNFSZ'T, Q'HH BQHH IQF. QP
QJ'T FQZR, Q'HH BQHH FMTRHP.

　　　　　　　—ZRQH TQFNZ

　　　　　　　43

173. AM UHGYZD GRIW AZ HII HSRBG
GYZ STDWJ HPW GYZ SZZJ, GYZ
ITHD—T KZPG JGZHWM KTGY H
KRRWCZVQZD GTII T KHJ GKZPG-RPZ.

—SRS YRCZ

174. SVTCP TWN RV IXPUNEVCVI DKV
VFTUD BNXAD, DKV IVTI UVADVC, NJ
ZXIIMV TWV. XD NUUQCP RKVA SNQ TCV
DNN SNQAW DN DTYV QB WNMJ
TAI DNN NMI DN CQPK QB DN DKV AVD.

—JCTAYMXA B. TITZP

175. GBX'Y VEZZA E VEX YB ZQMBZV
CRV—YCEY'K OCEY ZQMBZV KNCBBDK
EZQ MBZ.   —VEQ OQKY

176. DPZ GQAVD DQBZ THM WMT K
PHMVZ THM VZZ PHJ YAZDDT DPZ
YKQED QV KEO WMT QD. DPZ VZRHEO
DQBZ THM FHHS DH VZZ QG DPZ
WKVZBZED PKV DZABQDZV. QD'V DPZ
VKBZ JQDP BZE.   —FMYZ XZFZL

44

177. D MDTKIZ OEK XPNZ WXZ FPUZ
LXPRLZ EM SDRRDRT WXZ GEWWZIO
SXZWXZI OEK JGPO EI REW.

                  —MIPR GZAESDWQ

178. HUR GYE XYZF EGFU CYK ZLQ
VTYKM HUR EHSFM SYNFSGFM CYK
NFS NTKF. HUR SGFU CYK HRR FNNP
HUR PKNHM HUR CYK NFS XHJF.
EGFMF RYFP SGF NTKF NY?

                  —MLSH MKRUFM

179. CN UOA CRMFEA ULV CH UOA
STCMA KFI OLZA UF SLK UF DAAS UOA
BFZATREARU FR CUH NAAU, LQCEFRK
CH UOA STCMA JA OLZA UF SLK NFT
HJAASCRB L JFELR FNN OATH.

                  —BTFIMOF ELTV

180. VSP HYGHSP GI VKMP. CPX YGFP
HBKI BXA JTCPX YGFP HYTVSPI. G TXYO
YGFP HBKI EPHBMIP VSPO VBFP CP VT
HYTVSPI.   —KGVB KMAXPK

181. Q OTV'K DFYQFLF XJV QR
GTXJV'R VJKBNJY FVFXC. ZFNSJZR SQR
YJGCFN QR.   —RSJVJ JYFEJVOFN

182. CMH PRMJ, ZC BFS BLDS CMH
VSNUF DC NAS, CMH'KS DNXS GOSRBC
MQ DLEBNPSE LQ CMH'KS OLKSX CMHV
OLQS GVMGSVOC.   —VMRNOX VSNANR

183. EZJUJ'G X EHNJ LZJQ WYC ZXIJ EY
JRKMXHQ EY WYCU SZHMOUJQ LZW
EZJW'UJ VYUQ, XQO HE'G X
NXUIJMYCG EZHQD HT WYC FQYL EZJ
UJXGYQ VW EZJQ.   —ZXPJM GSYEE

184. AJCETZQVVN, D XFDZB DH Q ITYQZ
FQEZ'X YJX XFJ CDSFX YQZ ON XFJ
XDYJ EFJ'E XIJZXN-HTPC, EFJ
YQN OJ VPMBN.   —LJOTCQF BJCC

185. O VTQW T JTQ VCF'Z BOQP TQP
XQPILZWTQPOQR. OZ WCTW WFF JXKC
WF TZB FN T JOHHOFQTOLI?
                    —UZT UZT RTSFL

186. M LDUSUD HOU PKDW
"OKGUGYCUD" ZUXYJFU "OKJFUPMSU"
YEPYTF MGLEMUF HOYH HOUDU GYT ZU
Y PMSU FKGULEYXU UEFU.

—ZUEEY YZVJQ

187. G MBUUVMP FEPW KEPJ QPRZE R
ZPQKRGW RCP MVXP XPW RQP RAQRGY
KV CQVF BU. GK MPPXM KEP VOYPQ
KEP XPW CPK, KEP JVBWCPQ KEPGQ
WPF FGDPM CPK.

—POGNRTPKE KRJOVQ

188. WQV ILFPTB YLHGR MTBULBI FPT
CLZD LU DTJTBWG WAB-FBWUUAY
YLQFBLGGTBD NAFP TWDT.

—GADW WGFPTB

189. LYOI YO TF EXHO QSD MTIIOD
XIM T CISL YO GJFH RO OTHYOD
YXNTIZ XI XQQXTD SD EVTIZ MOXM TI
HYO FHDOOH, T XELXVF YSWO YO'F
MOXM.

—AJMTHY NTSDFH

190. QV BVY LFSIT UB USIQ SX
UCLYKSIR HCLZ, VK XSUJHB KVLLZQ
ZCKHB?   —VRQZI ICXF

191. TIFXG FU GZJ CEFNJ MJ CRQ
MFXXFATXQ HYE LYFAT MZRG MJ REJ
TYFAT GY LY RAQMRQ.

                         —FURPJXXJ ZYXXRAL

192. LJASBCJ ZM CDBQCM MJRQA WH
QJAJRQND BUCW CDJ HJZBUBUJ AWEV,
B DRGJ UWC MJC PJJU RPVJ CW
RUAIJQ... CDJ FQJRC YEJACBWU CDRC
DRA UJGJQ PJJU RUAIJQJL: IDRC
LWJA R IWZRU IRUC?

                         —ABFZEUL HQJEL

193. A'V CKMMZ KIKAJ AP A PLXJV K
CKJ YFL FKV PAPEOOJ CARRALJ
VLRRKMB KJV YLXRV BAIJ LQOM FKRP
LP AE EL CO TOPLMO EFO CKMMAKIO,
KJV IXKMKJEOO FO'V TO VOKV YAEFAJ
EFO ZOKM.   —TOEEO VKQAB

194. MFGC WSFPY PG ZOK KSOYPKKE
Z OSFA EKKIH OGGI BZFKEPH. MFGC
KSOYPKKE PG PYSFPV-MSLK HYK EKKIH
OGGI AGGTH. MFGC PYSFPV-MSLK PG
MSMPV-MSLK HYK EKKIH Z OGGI
BKFHGEZASPV. MFGC MSMPV-MSLK GE,
HYK EKKIH OGGI QZHY.

—HGBYSK PNQTKF

195. ZX TXWTJ PMPE GJXXIG VWGDPIG
OHIJ JHG ABWSPEG. SXK FKGI RXZ'I
OWZI IJPY IX PMPE DZXO IJWI SXK
TWZ'I GJXXI.   —VXVVS DZHLJI

196. EBFS N VNS QYFSX N JNO HQQO
PQO BRX ERPF, RM'X FRMBFO N SFE
JNO QO N SFE ERPF.

—YORSJF YBRURY

197. XBB KJP KJHYLI H GPXBBU BHDP
KA RA XGP PHKJPG HZZAGXB,
HBBPLXB, AG NXKKPYHYL.

—XBPSXYRPG QAABBTAKK

198. J ABQR MLR "TOCX XABDTR"
JCZNR. J LZQR DBMLJDN MB AJQR OE
MB.   —EZCRAZ TRDJKR ZDTRIKBD

199. NYAFA XP HEA NYXES X JHQRZ
TFABG QM HOAF, BEZ NYBN XP XC PYA
IBQSYN KA JXNY BEHNYAF JHKBE. X
JHE'N PNBEZ CHF NYBN.

                    —PNAOA KBFNXE

200. KLIZJ TNZ NZMZTDZXGP TUUFBZX
LQ DTEAJY DVAJYB MZNBLJTGGP. A
UTJJLD BZZ TJP LDVZN VLJZBD KTP
LQ DTEAJY DVZI.   —ITNPT ITJJZB

201. BXWE XV EJU EDBU D IXO'E JMTU
BCFJ VCO. EJU YUWE XV EJU EDBU D
IXO'E JMTU MOP VCO ME MAA.

                    —KXXIP MAAUO

202. QTYBU ETJUN YTL GTYYSXZ TYU
TGGUWXTVQU TZ MSSN SEQK XS XISZU
LIS QACU AE IRXGIUZ UTBUYQK
TLTAXAEB UTZXUY.   —MYTE QUVSLAXH

203. HYWXBFHYQFOEJ, DXGOFZGOD
VOXVEO MXY'F UOQB JXH HYFZE JXH
DKBOQG.   —DFOWQYZO VXNOBD

204. MLK MW DZK NGKXD AEDJ MW
XYY DEFK AXJ DZK BKGJML AZM
RXYYKI DZKF KXJU BXUFKLDJ.

                    —NKMGNK TSGLJ

205. ZSR ORPYL DRZNRRW TGTZO PWE
LRARWZO PYR ZSR SPYERLZ. OJM PYR
PVNPOL DRGWF PLHRE ZJ EJ ZSGWFL,
PWE OJM PYR WJZ ORZ ERQYRXGZ
RWJMFS ZJ ZMYW ZSRI EJNW.

                    —Z.L. RVGJZ

206. ER VUSZ IQ HKBSFNIEZG VH
HIESIGS NMI HWFKXH MSF ING
QCIIFH.   —XSJJS EVUCSF

207. WGMDUWVKL UZ G ADVTJZZ HL
RIUTI G XDVTJD GTFPUDJZ GK
GTTVPKM MIJ YSVDUZM IGC.

                    —YDGKTUZ DVCWGK

208. WKH RQOB WLPH WR EHOLHYH DQB
NLQG RI UDWLQJ LV ZKHQ LW VKRZV
BRX DW WKH WRS.   —ERE KRSH

209. OPEXKDXPPV MQ EXK OPQE
KOPEMPBIA KGCKDMKBJK PW PBK'Q
AMWK. PBK YPMBQ I NMBV PW
SPOKB'Q OIWMI.   —YIBKE QRHOIB

210. ILSYUVIJW AIPS QSSJ
VGJBUXUGJSB XG YSWMSVX JSNJSWW,
NAIXSPSY UX VGWXW XASL.

                        —EGAJ FMBUCS

211. B SMYHGM ZE KXDBZ ZNKZ B'D
DESM ZNKQ YBYZJ-ZIE MTMQ BY ZNKZ
XEMG DKCM DJ GEQG BPPMABZBDKZM.
                        —PKXJ KGZES

212. VFEFY PFFZ YFUSYOF PSY GBNA
KSC BNEF ABSCDBA NLSCA KSCY GRPF;
OBF BNO ABSCDBA UCJB GSYOF
ABRVDO NLSCA KSC.   —XFNV YSOANVH

52

213. Z YZTXGPUW KGRGW BMCJG VGJF
URGW JXG CAGZ JXZJ XG CF Z JXCKV
UL YGZMJI ZKA Z YUI LUWGRGW.

—XGPGK WUSPZKA

214. NIANYI EWA YKQI KM JYGCC
WADCIC CWADYU NDYY PWI TYKMUC
EWIM OIZAQKMJ PWIKO POADCIOC.

—CNKLI ZKYYKJGM

215. CG TNAAFB SGP SNDDZYO N PGTNC
TNO RF TNBBZFI, ZA NYPNOL DYFNLFL
SFB AG IZLMGUFB ASNA ASFBF ZL N
CZMF TNC PSG PZLSFL ASNA LSF PFBF
CGA.   —S.Y. TFCMHFC

216. K IVHR ZO ZSZVKAI VU ZO HVMS
HKUS GV JDAYSA FAVGWSAI DXR
GWSO DAS LVKXL GV ZDYS D LDZS
VNG VU KG.   —CVVRO DHHSX

217. XU'N VYU FMRUMRJ AYD FXV YJ
OYNR—XU'N MYF AYD OEA UMR IOEZR.

—SJEV ORIYFXUB

218. F ETBQ BX USZQTM ZWYXZU—IWB
AETB QRUQ DTO XOQ MX AFBE BEQY?

—TYTOMT RQTZ

219. NYX QXVBYR AY QADX GN MXXU
RAQXYG VYJ JBVI NYX'R NIY
ONYDERANYR.   —ONBYXQAV NGAR
RMAYYXB

220. J MJLF KBZ MFOP, BOE BT B
NBUUFS PG GBDU, IF JT WFSZ
DPODFSOFE BCPVU NZ IFBMUI. JO
GBDU, IF JOTJTUFE UIBU J KPH
UISPVHI DFOUSBM QBSL BCPVU
NJEOJHIU UPOJHIU.   —KPIOOZ DBSTPO

221. X DROM QP NPQMH. X WPQ'J MOMQ
DROM R FROXQYF RVVPBQJ SMVRBFM X
WPQ'J AQPI NH NPN'F NRXWMQ QRNM.
                    —CRBUR CPBQWFJPQM

222. X QBCXD QHKJBMK X CXD HI
AHFP X NHIJ QHKJBMK X VHTUTAP.
                    —LABGHX IKPHDPC

223. PNNJVSHH IST JCN NP JIR CNETJ
PRSJWERT NP SFREQXSZ HQPR:
AQNHRZXR TRUSESJRK VM XNFFQJJRR
FRRJQZYT.   —YRNEYR CQHH

224. LRR W MLTA QD YLG LODIQ EAP
LPV OLQMFDDEY WY... QMAG'FA PDQ
FALR YZAKWSWK.   —FWQL FIVPAF

225. RYLZL AF PDRYAPM CDZL
WLQZLFFAPM RYJP RD ZLJW RYL OAFR
DX RYL CDFR QDQGOJZ FRDOLP
SLYAKOLF DX OJFR ILJZ JPW PDR XAPW
IDGZ KJZ OAFRLW.

                           —LZCJ VDCVLKB

226. YOHHM FT O POX LFAY O LFKZ AB
AZCC YFP LYOA AB GB OXG O
TZWDZAODM AB GB FA.

                           —CBDG POXWDBKA

227. YLQGQ WGQ YLGQQ YLJEMI J'KQ
PQY YB SB: BDQGW, GBSQB, WES
DBGEB.   —VQW WGYLZG

228. QMAFA LFA QJD FALYDPY JMG W
LE YIKKAYYSIR WP YMDJ OIYWPAYY, LPV
W LE YQLPVWPC DP ODQM DS QMAE.

      —OAQQG CFLORA

229. YCK-OWFSUYGMK TYCUHUIWC
IWGKUKWHM: YGM LSYFM QWD QUCCF
MJIMMK SUF EMKUW WKNMDHUFUGZ
QPKZMH.   —LMGKMCC HDYZKYG

230. DG KRE R KZYRU KFZ MCZIJ YJ
GZ MCDUX, RUM D UJIJC FRM GFJ
TZNCGJEO GZ GFRUX FJC HZC DG.

      —K.T. HDJWME

231. ZSOH-LSVSZHJ FVPOOHO PZH
YHEHZ UPJH BY NBRSLPVO. YSNSJK
GPYAO AS ZHPJ ADH OUPVV QZBYA BY
JZHPUO.   —PYY VPYJHZO

232. SMJAXPA CQAJ XQN ESVA NUA
UASTN KTQH GQXCAT, MYN WN JYTA
UASNJ YZ NUA MRQQC.

     —ARWOSMANU SJURAL

233. ERU HBWH O'Q RIYG TOJHV, O'Q
IYYGOEN HRUWGMT GYTFYXHWLODOHV.
          —TBYDDYV UOEHYGT

234. OR UGJ ZFW ZAA LFZBBWX JB OE
UGJFHWAR, UGJ ZFW GSWFXFWHHWX.
          —VZIW PZASWFHGE

235. YD'E G TUUA DWYQT DWGD
NVGXDP YE UQFP EZYQ AVVJ UL Y'A
NV LUDDVQ DU DWV BULV
          —JWPFFYE AYFFVL

236. W TZHD ZY Z REKIH'F TZHD. WY'F
BMEFIA YXLII EL SENL AZUF Z KEHYX
ANI YE BLZKQF.   —GNAU BZLYIL

237. P OEVPF OWE KPF KETI ORBW
BWI BIXXRUQI BOEZ KPF KETI ORBW
PFHBWRFA.   —GLMRBW KQPUIZ

238. C QCF DF PHXG DZ DFJHQNPGLG
OFLDP BG BCZ QCYYDGT. LBGF BG'Z
WDFDZBGT.   —IZC IZC SCAHY

239. GV NL QPGFHPJ KZEJSREHGZ ET
RPKOUPHST. LBLHDVQL GPOLT SHFWT
GVSPD LIKLXG UZLQ GZLD QLLS GZLN.

—HEGP HFSQLH

240. GO HDJR SDMRIUF QYLR YEPYOF
TMLRI GR HQYH FJKDRGR KDNNS NS
URLNHMNI, Y FKNIHYIRNJF YLRDFMNI
SND HQR GYI M ENLRU.   —XNERHHR

241. R OFVMGY YIMHG'J QI IG R YVMJ
KMXRNHM UIN RFM ORJ. R OFVMGY
GMLMF YMOMGYH R ZNHKRGY PZI QMJH
ZVH PVOM RG MCMXJFVX
HAVCCMJ OIF ZMF KVFJZYRU. R
OFVMGY PVCC JMCC UIN HZM HRP UINF
ICY KIUOFVMGY—RGY ZM'H R BFVMHJ.

—MFER KIEKMXA

242. SU GV JMLUJV-IRHQJ WRHJPAZV
GV IZJPLH QZRA, "QSU, PLHL'Q Z
GRYYRSU ASYYZHQ. ASU'J YSQL RJ."

—YZHHV URCLU

243. PXN JZDM KEVRS FEPB EC FPGBX
UZM SVGGCM ZGRJ VU EC'X LDJVGA.

                —UMPG RCLZFVBQ

244. LBA EZXL RIOWAHZNX KZHR PO
LBA AOWVPXB VIOWNIWA PX
AXLPEILA... CAFINXA AXLPEILA
CIXPFIVVM EAIOX FBIDLAH AVASAO.

                —HPLI HNROAH

245. U QXYGCJ SZ ECSYGCJ MXMRO EXJ
FJXBK, PCMUBZC ZGC REXDZ YGC
ZMGXXV FJSEMSFUV QUO MUVV UY UEO
QSEBYC YX JCFXJY YGUY GCJ MGSVK
GUZ WBZY KJSLCE U
QXYXJMOMVC YGJXBIG YGC
IOQEUZSBQ.   —QUJO RUO PVURCVO

246. YB XWSSIU NBQ ABGL DS DJ
BCSJDLI, YIOIU RB DYSB W GDHCBU
JSBUI QIWUDYR W JZD XWJZ.

                —"PWUACJ,"
       QWDJRGWJJ WYL ABCGSNWUS

247. CDP KBXM JPFUKB N OKVXI CFGP
VH WKTTNBT NU UK N LKVXI DPFJ
DPFSM AJPFCDNBT FTFNB.

—PJZF AKZAPLG

248. HJOG KG KD HLWT FWBRA, TZGAU
EJZ, EXS E RGEBNJTBW YEZNXGZ, EXS
DLB FEX IGGY KD HLWT FWBRA EXS
NUG TZGAU EJZ.   —VEFI RGXXD

249. IT NBO ENTDGPZAO KVZO RN
VFT, "P GZFO QBFTENT DNG RYZ
FGRPWBZV." P KVZO RN VFT, "GPCYR, P
CN RN VYNQQPAC IFBBV DNG RYZ
IKVPW."   —GPRF GKOAZG

250. XUF ZFNCXU T HXU'Q HZTUV TC
QDNQ T INUQ QX VUXI IDFU T'W
DNGTUR N RXXH QTWF.   —YNHM NCQXZ

251. BAXW HJ V QHEW. ZRG UKWGKWE
HG HJ IAHFI GA UVEN PARE KWVEGK AE
ZREF YAUF PARE KARJW, PAR TVF
FWXWE GWBB.   —DAVF TEVUQAEY

60

252. XW MPNON L HAON DQO L
JOQUNS PNLOM? QSTI MXZN HLS PNLT
IQAO JOQUNS PNLOM, RAWM LW MXZN
HLS PNLT PXW JOQUNS LOZW LSF
TNBW.   —ZXWW VXBBI

253. TE TNZCP-HAEECP OYCCVM
OMJKDH XC DAGC T DTHI'O HPCOO—
DJEQ CEJKQM ZJ VJBCP ZMC OKXSCVZ
TEH OMJPZ CEJKQM ZJ XC
AEZCPCOZAEQ.   —P.T. "PTX" XKZDCP

254. JPGYVBSG VLZ DOFZ KOLZG.
IJZW MC CPI XJZB PBVIIZBSZS.
                      —QGV QGV MVYCL

255. MJ CSY AERX WSQIXLMRK HSRI
AIPP, KIX E GSYTPI SJ SPH FVSEHW
XS HS MX.   —FIXXI HEZMW

256. ILRER JG ZW ADRXGKER JZ
LXMJZN ZWILJZN IW TW; ILR PKZ JG
JZ LXMJZN DWIG IW TW XZT ZWI
TWJZN JI.   —BXES CJDGWZ DJIIDR

257. KLR KLJZN QABRZ LYOR NAK KA
DRYGZ JI KLYK ZAWATU NJORI UAM
CAQRG. UAM HMIK KYFR JK.

—GAIRYZZR WYGG

258. AVTU H FZ BZ BVT NTRPBJ
ERYXZPY, H RXARJK PKT BVT
TCTYFTUIJ TUBYRUIT. KZCTBHCTK H
SPKB FZ WZY RU TKBHCRBT.

—EVJXXHK MHXXTY

259. AQW PGXGT TGCNKBG JQY UJQTV
C OQPVJ KU WPVKN AQW RCA
CNKOQPA.   —LQJP DCTTAOQTG

260. Z WZRXIKLB'C HDBSTI UIVIGUC
TVLG XDC ZKIBSGICC; Z YZBBDIU YZG'C
UIVIGUC TVLG XDC QDNI'C.

—X.K. YIGRMIG

261. J'QR ZDSZWK XRDJRQRT JA MLR
ZTZNR MLZM MLR KRVIRM CP RMRIAZD
WCOML JK ZIIRKMRT TRQRDCEBRAM.

—ZDJVR ICCKRQRDM DCANSCIML

262. OUG NUX'E HLE UILA VTEFXH EU
PUUB, TXO WUAL EVTX OUG HLE UILA
VTIFXH RFH JLLE.   —ZLH RATPBLX

263. F SQXABGRLBK ELJGXL RA
ELILSB ZK SHL. PUSR SZ F? S OSE?
                         —OKYMF BSGTLE

264. S HWAYMLSC WO S LSZ QJM
SYQSRO BULULGUBO S QMLSZ'O
GWBCJHSR GPC ZUDUB BULULGUBO JUB
SVU.   —BMGUBC IBMOC

265. J XLZD OVH TJUUHNHLGH
SHODHHL F IZZT YFL FLT F SFT ZLH,
SCO J VFPHL'O THGJTHT DVJGV J
KJXH SHOOHN.   —YFH DHBO

266. BU TJCMTP MA DMZP QYI PMKJPN
KC VP Y EMYAC EDYUPN MA Y
QJCNPJCLIP CN Y ECDMKMTMYA. YAR KC
KPDD UCL KJP KNLKJ, KJPNP'I
JYNRDU YAU RMZZPNPATP.
                     —JYNNU I KNLBYA

267. IJP QXI X DCOPDU LHGD. CMG
TCMGKIJHY QXI NXIK XBR NMGHCMI—H
QXI NXIK XBR IJP QXI NMGHCMI.

—AXS ZXMNNAXBB

268. YSD UIZDUN YSFVE OCILY CDFVE
QIXYN FK YSOY NIL POV OWWXDPFOYD
YMDVYN-QFZD-NDOX-IUR HDV HIXD.

—PIUUDDV HPPLUUILES

269. F BZUL T YUN UJ AMUAYM VFVZ'N
MOAMPN UIE EMYTNFUZGXFA NU YTGN—
RIN LM'KM DIGN PMYMRETNMV UIE NLU
WUZNXG' TZZFKMEGTEQ.

—REFNN MBYTZV

270. V LAY'G EJJ ZINF AH RBHUJL
RYQ ZAUJ EVYNJ FJ TAG EA
VYGJUJEGJL VY EJO.

—ZUE. RBHUJL XVYEJQ

271. KBX GUEKSO XKUZRN KPLS
EKOUYA KBG PYPV PAN HSQE EKS
XEUOH.

—GPS YSXE

64

272. K ICAFP UM UGW IKG RW DKOSCD
GUD DU PU IWBDKAG DCAGSL LOIC KL
DUOIC K CUD LDUNW, DOBG UG DCW
SKL, YOFF FKJYL UMM DCWAB DKRFWL
RH DCWAB IUBPL, UB XKTW JUJJH
RWMUBW GUUG.   —QUKG BANWBL

273. HA EOH WC JFXZMOJ WH LWC
OYYFHTOHDF OY YLF LAZCF AK
DAEEAHC ZHYWM LF WC EOJJWFT.
                    —PFHROEWH TWCJOFMW

274. KAQD Y KPLYD WQMMT ZPB AQE
YVQ, OW'T YMM EOVAW WP MPPI
TBEREOTQS, UBW SPD'W TNPKM.
                    —KOMTPD LOCDQE

275. ZVUPH ZBHK UPH, QBJPPJX,
UVHPA, QESGCJPH, DJSPHCX,
GYMYJA, QVUDVJK, SHCPIPHCPHQP,
DJPPCVU, JPXIPQK, GVLP BHC B KEJPP-
CVGGBJ IBHKAEVXP KEBK
ZVH'K JYH.   —IEAGGSX CSGGPJ

276. MW CXG PXID EXADXKD, EDO
OUDA WJDD. MW OUDC SXAD RQSL,
OUDC'JD HJXRQRPC RJXLD.

—JUXKVQ VMSLEMXK

277. HZ HIPBO'D H KEG FWB, LV GBE
HLZ'P PHYMLZK HTBEP WLA, HLZ'P
YLDPJZLZK.   —AHOYBZ TOHZUB

278. UZD TZVFJS XLVXJL WV VFG PQS
XPD GV TLL RPS MEJNT UZLQ GZLD KPQ
TGPD PG ZVNL PQS TLL RPS
GLJLBETEVQ MVH QVGZEQW?

—TPNFLJ WVJSUDQ

279. UL CJMB NULAJDL BWXUTC LAWL
XJD BAJDGI TMOMY AWOM FJYM
PAUGIYMT LAWT XJD AWOM PWY
NUTIJNB.   —MYFW KJFKMPQ

280. RMO, UD UIOUJD, XWK NMDX
UFXMNUXKV UGGIAURPK AR U W
MFDKWMIV AD XWK NMXWKB.

—LKHKBIJ EMRKD

66

281. J XLZW IR PTA UXPDFYJUBF.
YXWR XLZW IR JAJYJLQF PA YPD. LAG
ZWQUOP PA YXW SPYYPI.

                    —OJYL OVGAWO

282. W YOQPFAAQO RA QSF NBQ
CWUVA RS AQXFQSF FUAF'A AUFFY.

                    —N.B. WEHFS

283. VKS BQEF CP Q VEIS WEIGK... XG
VKQV LCI PQDD XA DCTS PXEGV QAN
OECYS PCE ESQGCAG QPVSEJQEN.

                    —GKQAQ QDSRQANSE

284. WOWM QCWM KDWGCYT QVGCWP
VMP DWYZWOWP NK VYY NUOZNHG
LNMKWLFZNMG, LCZYPDWM FWMP FN
UW GFZLET.   —KDVM YWUNQZFX

285. KFWWMFET MH FI FZZMFIRT
TIUTWTL MIUY GQ F KFI JXY RFI'U
HZTTO JMUX UXT JMILYJ HXAU, FIL F
JYKFI JXY RFI'U HZTTO JMUX UXT
JMILYJ YOTI.   —ETYWET GTWIFWL HXFJ

67

286. HL WZYM HT GVM UATRMX, QZIWO
PZI CWMUTM XMCVXUTM GVM
EIMTGHZA?   —WHWP GZBWHA

287. CBF NQC XP NJCRUD JXUARACA
RU TFFSRUD SFXSWF PQXV JXEDBRUD.
                —QNWSB QRJBNQHAXU

288. RITTLAZU I RIZ AB GAEQ KFLAZU
BYRQDWAZU LYF'HQ KQQZ IORATAZU
SYT I GYZU DARQ AZ I BWYX PAZOYP.
LYF RIL GYHQ AD PWQZ LYF UQD AD
WYRQ, KFD AD OYQBZ'D IGPILB UY
PADW QHQTLDWAZU QGBQ.
                        —CQIZ EQTT

289. WMSSEMAU EP XZB GDPB
PYESEBDMR QZWWDXEZX MXT
YMPPEZXMBU UWOSMQUP; WMSSEMAU
EP MRPZ BCSUU WUMRP M TMN,
PCMSEXA BCU HZSIRZMT MXT
SUWUWOUSEXA BZ QMSSN ZDB BCU
BSMPC.   —TS. GZNQU OSZBCUSP

68

290. JKIGD BQHNQB GB G RKKTWDO-
ORGBB CKBBQBBWDO XVQ IGOWY
CKJQHB KE HQERQYXWDO XVQ EWOSHQ
KE IGD GX XJWYQ WXB DGXSHGR BWPQ.
                    —NWHOWDWG JKKRE

291. PLKM QUO TKV XIAV EDEVQ, QUO
LIFK VU SKJDSK PLKVLKN VU YKKX
QUON EIJK UN QUON EDTONK. D YKXV
CQ EIJK.   —RINRINI JINVZIMS

292. S PCYW WX ACNL EASRTHLY PASRL
GK QCHLYWZ CHL ZWSRR
KXDYV LYXDVA WX WCFL ECHL XO
WALG.   —HSWC HDTYLH

293. EBJ ZAA OBCQE MKTQ CBIJ BN
JRQKG OZHKEM JRBWMRJI JB DAQZIKEM
CQE. IBCQ ZGQ CZGGKQS.
                    —QCCZ AQQ

294. SLRFRQRI WDO SZFM MD EZIIW
KDERDFR, ND LZQR COFVL SJML LJK
RU-SJPR.   —KLRCCRW SJFMRIK

69

295. PNOOXFM Y MGGC NIYTEAN QGL
WGBL HSXACLNF OYJNP YAA OSN QBF
GBO GQ TXCCAN YMN.

—RXAAXYT QNYOSNL

296. PITY QLO'AT FLATG PVBI
QLOANTXH, KRAAQ RYG FT FLATG
PVBI NLKTLYT TXNT.

—GRCVG ZAQST-WLYTN

297. COSXYO W UOR UB IPVCEJF, W'F
JOLOY SEKKOJ WJ KXLO.... W VRONNOF
WJ WR E SOQ RWUOV.   —YWRE YPFJOY

298. EWD DYJXDJE HYN GZQ NZCQ
MWXIFQDO EZ IDYQO YRZCE PZODN XJ
GZQ NZC OZE EZ WYKD YON.

—VYEWDQXOD HWXEDWZQO

299. EFD KJVVADM CFAYF H THX
SDWSDEM EFD TJME AX FAM VAKD HSD
EFJMD CFAYF FD OAOX'E YJTTAE
CFDX FD FHO EFD JBBJSELXAER.

—FDVDX SJCVHXO

300. U YDRKRD XZ KZDCRX PZXT
YGUDL ZK CMGLLRL GFI YGLL NO
IRAMUFUFC ORGDL LGMVXUFC LXDGFCR
JZNRF GFI CDGFIKGXTRD AMZAEL.

—ZCIRF FGLT

301. HZOEE HOQPE OZU OJJ CUZG LUJJ
KQ IAUKZ XJOVU—YRIPYYZE OQP
EUCUZOJ SKJUE OLOG.

—IAYSOE HUUVAOS

302. DEYMI, BG GONYMP EOG, HXW
MJXQGTI TBCM WMJ; IEO GSEOASG EZ
YEGSBYA MTWM BZ IEO PBPY'G SXKM
BG, XYP GSEOASG EZ EGSMN GSBYAW
BZ IEO PBP.   —RXDMW VXTPHBY

303. WBVJLHRMQHBM: LN HB RTDRVB
JRTTNI R YNQON BWNJHRTHBM
KNJRCBN HM BECYIB KNMMNQ, KCM
NONQVEYN GYEDB LN'B R BEQM EZ
PRYHMEQ HY R TEEYNV KHY.

—W.S. DEINLECBN

304. VIL DIQERNRTC NTC PYUQ IRE
SREVTHLE, PYV VIL TUNIRVLNV NTC
GCBQ TKXREL IRE NBRLCV VG DBTCV
XRCLE.   —ZUTCH BBGQK MURJIV

305. J QEPB LQB ZWLBYLJEV LW SB
JYDNBMJSVU WNTEYJRBM.
KYOWNLKYELBVU, HU WNTEYJRELJWY
VEDAI DWYIJILBYDU.   —QBVBY YEIQ

306. MZYKA YO ONLPKAYDR KAZK UNG
QPCYPJP KAZK DNQNSU YD AYO FYRAK
LYDS XNGCS QPCYPJP.
                    —ZFVAYP QGDWPF

307. UWCHFSKBKICWQW QW
WUZBNQBO YSXEC NSIIKXW KB FSRX ES
WLRZKI SB CSRX PSEFZX.
                    —PQAZ HSBBSIIC

308. C ICYY SANAW PA US FYX EUS.
LF EA, FYX UBA CZ UYIUJZ QCQLAAS
JAUWZ FYXAW LTUS C UE.
                    —PAWSUWX PUWHMT

309. F LQBNP UPI UB OFOUPPI
DFYWJL W KWG. WU QG WYP F XWTP UB
XBZK BI UB LBQPUXFIY.

                    —YPBJYP HEJIL

310. TWJFVRT JUB VH UVYP APVRT
VRNWPLHVRTUE ZPRLUVMPB CJW L
NWVKP EJG DLQPR'S NJKKVSSPB.

                    —LRSDJRE ZJFPUU

311. IGRNP YQNXNQ RNP IVG VJBN
ZGRNOVTPW ONPENQ JHGFO OVNR—
NZYNSTJMML OVN MNWJM CTPE.

                    —CJL TPWQJR

312. KIJ MZZ, AZNB, SR SM WIR RBJZ
RGNR VIENW VNM ENAZ YBIE ENW'M
BSO; MGZ VNM BZNXXK ENAZ YBIE
GSM YJWWK OIWZ.   —L.E. ONBBSZ

313. WML HFTNLIDRV WMKYA FZDRW F
XDSL PKWM F EDRZIL HLFYKYA KV
WMFW KW OFY DYIQ HLFY DYL WMKYA.

                    —TDYYKL ZFTSLT

73

314. LEJNUODXZOEX: D BDW RUY
DESE JYV D AYX YQ MPLMWEOGM
TVMEXOYWE JYVZ ROQM DESE JYV
QYZ WYXUOWF.   —EDB KDZHMAA

315. KTH CLWF R KLARS KLDN QWS
HWRDF QL PTRSUW R ARS'F TRMOQF
RSC QTWS PLAZVROS QTRQ TW'F SLQ
QTW ARS FTW ARDDOWC?

              —MRDMDR FQDWOFRSC

316. AWD OVY EMXMXSME LIMD OVY
GQGD'U LWDU UV JZMMT? QJD'U QU
QDAVDAMQFWSZM? Q PYMJJ UIM
GMBQDQUQVD VB WGYZUIVVG QJ UIWU
OVY LWDU UV JZMMT.

              —TWYZW TVYDGJUVDM

317. BESKS XT Y UYTB ZXQQSKSCNS
ASBFSSC BES TYUYHS YCZ BES
NXUXGXDSZ JYC, APB XB XT CSUSK
YMMYKSCB BR BESXK FXUST PCBXG
YQBSK AKSYVQYTB.   —ESGSC KRFGYCZ

318. WSCGQB SNSYO LJAASLLIJD
VKHXQ... GL X LJWLFXQFGXD XHKJQF KI
AKIISS.   —LFSECXQGS EGYK

319. W TQS QJ WH WCAUQHWVQAH MHVA
VBS TAGK WHK W XSGP
FGSJSHV BSTF QH VGAMCTS.
                          —WKTWQ JVSXSHJAH

320. OM LCZ WKKA ZCON MLCM C
WJONK'Z CMMOMXNK MTDCJNZ LKJ
WKMJTMLKN SCA WK ZXHHKN XG OA
MLJKK DTJNZ: COZEK. CEMCJ. LRHA.
                          —YJCAU HXOJ

321. X CGR'Y UMTR YG SDGB GMC
SDTLJENMMZ. X UMTR YG OTIJ ETLJ-
MXEYP YXMM FZ JTDP FJJY.
                          —DXYT DNCRJD

322. KQT DVQZ OR'G YBJI RQ YLBJ
ZYBR B ALBJILI CBV OG GBKOVU. YL
SBV'R GWLBD BAQHL B ZYOGDLJ.
                          —YLJCBV X. CBVDOLZOSN

75

323. UA HAKF AIF ZTWFIU, BW.
RAWUXDIE, BTM VF WFETWPFP TK T
BDKOAWUNIF; UA HAKF VAUX HAACK
HDCF GTWFHFKKIFKK. —AKGTW RDHPF

324. DPZEUN QCI: DQ OCF UCBN UEXN
MDCXF ERQ EW CUNXDZCP SNESMN
QOCP VEMW.   —KDMM XEVNXF

325. Z MVSCZW DHJUSZDU RPJ'U
GHSUF UFV KZKVS RU'P GSRUUVJ HJ.
                —PZQOVW BHWXGNJ

326. NPHDJIHBJD PX SZXHNL IQZBH
YIKPRF XDA IRV RZH SBTY IQZBH
YIKPRF TYPNVJDR; NPMD PX HYD ZHYDJ
CIL JZBRV.   —VIKPV NZVFD

327. FV KXW RFHQ RXOP QOXWPE,
BEQ HQOQZTIFRFBK VTDBXZ DZQQSU
FO; KXW PQB TDDWUQM XV BEFOPU
KXW OQHQZ MFM TOM SZTFUQM VXZ
HFZBWQU KXW OQHQZ ETM.
                —F.V. UBXOQ

328. CH FGSFJG YGIZMGU CK VIG PZQ
KZVCSKE US, VIGQ PSDJU ZJJ YG FDV
CK EVWZCVRZXBGVE.

—VGKKGEEGG PCJJCZAE

329. SC SK QYCCYL CG MVRY UGVTYI
VEI UGKC CMVE EYRYL CG MVRY
UGVTYI VC VUU.   —ZVPYK CMJLQYL

330. ASRD ASM WQS TS Q ULAFZQSX TZ
Q RMQXMG AY WMS—ULM AULMG STSM
LFSXGMX STSMUD-STSM YARRAV
VAWMS.   —EGAFJLA WQGO

331. GDMZ DF P WIPTZVO SXZR FZZR
DR LGEFZ-KJ, AKW P LEUZVO DR
GERT-FXEW.   —LXPIGDZ LXPJGDR

332. BD WSDDE GT WDEYLYUD LVVPW,
BD IYCD OGTTDL YEYLU, BD UYXD
WDEYLYUD CYJYUGVTW—BD'LD OVGTH
DCDLRUIGTH BD JYT UV XDDE VQL
PYLLGYHD UVHDUIDL.

—LVOTDR OYTHDLKGDSO

333. NYZR CRYCOR ENP UMR NRQJRU
YS YDJ OYVW ZEJJXEWR. FR UEPR UXZR
UY WY UY E JRNUEDJEVU UFY UXZRN E
FRRP. E OXUUOR QEVGOROXWMU
GXVVRJ, NYSU ZDNXQ EVG GEVQXVW.
NMR WYRN UDRNGEAN, X WY SJXGEAN.
                  —MRVVA AYDVWZEV

334. T DKQDBE EDB D OTVK GFEL OIL
GDVVTIN SPV KPRI—DZN UIIY PZ
OILLTZO GDVVTIN FZLTK EAI STZNE TL.
                  —CED CED ODJPV

335. W BIDVL SZRC PZSDLZB W ADDP
EKSP.... HDT BZZ, LIZ EZBBWAZB AD
XTKRCZV LD LIZ GVWKS GZRWTBZ
LIZH'JZ BIDVLZV LD AD.
                  —ETVKZF BNWVC

336. HIFMISF QH LTSK MTUWXQFY— MIR
WFEK JCTF QR QH TLTF. WFT
XIHR MT UPSTBIE FWR RW EWWZ EQZT
P XQNTA YSQEE.   —FWTE UWJPSA

337. Q DMFME HDML LIWU EMWZ
IWTTQDMJJ LWJ YDUQZ Q PVU
XWEEQMG. WDG SO UIMD QU LWJ UVV
ZWUM.   —XWN HWYBBXWDD

338. GI G CXB HO DGIS FK DGNS
XTXGQ, G'B HXPS FCS LXHS HGLFXPSL
KQDO LKKQSY.   —FXDDJDXC WXQPCSXB

339. X JRWGZ LGRITMJPLJRLJ. XY XP
YOJ UTDY YOTY FTAJP YOJ XMMRJPP
BGDYOBOXMJ.
                    —SJGDSJ VJDRTDC POTB

340. L BYP'R BUZUKFU RWLZ, OAR L
WQFU QKRWKLRLZ, QPB L BYP'R
BUZUKFU RWQR ULRWUK.
                    —MQDG OUPPH

341. Y DYNNVT HF WYZNL AYZB CPT
NHQDVT HF WYZNL MYACZVLLV QP LXV
NCHV TCF. Y XCJVP'L XCT LYHV WQZ
LQRCMMQ NYPMV.
                    —CZLIZQ LQNMCPYPY

342. UPOM XF NBVD QXVMK JP SM XQ
JDRQ RQ RBJPNPSXUM RVVXWMQJ, R
JXYDJ YXKWUM, R DXYDMK JRE
SKRVAMJ PK R DPUWXQY CRJJMKQ
POMK CDXURWMUCDXR.

—ZBWXJD OXPKFJ

343. MEJI RWMM HIJIL TI WAIZM NHYWM
KZH LIBEJILF SLEK YXI
WMMNFWEH YXZY XI BZH TI GNFY Z
MWYYMI TWY SZWYXSNM EL Z MWYYMI
TWY KZLLWIA.   —XIMIH LERMZHA

344. OUDJD QJD XKPC QRXGO OTDKOC
AGJVDJE Q CDQJ MK PXKVXK QKV AQKC
KXO QO QPP EDJMXGE—EXAD QJD FGEO
UGERQKVE LMPPMKY OUDMJ TMIDE.

—SXAAQKVDJ Y.U. UQOUDJMPP

345. RWUH ZQH HYA ZWYAJBP'R ZQH
PYRWLPT QOYAR RWU BUQB APJUZZ
LR'Z TYYB. WU'Z BUQB. TYYB.

—IYIZ IQOJUH

346. TJ JGORW G KBBF FRGN BI
ZYDWTQGN QBXEGKR JB ETFR G
YBEWR. JYTW, YBSRARE, T YGAR. T KRJ
TJ GJ GMBXJ IBEJD QRUJW G INGWO,
GUF JGOR TJ GW ERPXTERF.

                    —WJRZYRU NRGQBQO

347. OIQ VC XOSBIAY UZIOMMC
SBOMZHB AJOA Z'V LZQIOXXBQ OIQ
AJBC YIOX ZIAP OTAZPI
ZVVBQZOABMC: AJBC SBIA PKA VC
SPPV.   —RPPQC OMMBI

348. VSVX ACWJIC Q XJUGVP WK
EVWETV CQSV APRVM, XW WXV CQY LVA
KWJXM Q HQL AW MPRXN KWP Q
TRSRXI.   —OVQX NVPP

349. P UGF KIJOK TZ DJOLGFH FNK KN
WGMM GOMYYC NF G CJLMPU
CMGKWNIT, GFH DY JOJGMMZ UMGCO PF
KDY IPBDK CMGUYO.

                    —TGIBGIYK KDGKUDYI

81

350. Y'JV TVMYTVT LXCL UVZXCUN Y'H
RIBYHYM CPT OINL DVVU WQZAVLLYPA
LQ UIZAV. —UCIBC UQIPTNLQPV

351. KJKXDFEOD UNBKZ WK FKGNHZK
Q'W ZE HRQJKXZNIID IQSKO.
—TKBKX OK JXQKZ

352. CMXA XA L BJII OGTZCJN,
WLULW. RI MLEI L JXDMC CG AMLJI
NGTJ VJXELON XZ L VTQFXO VFLOI.
—VICIJ TACXZGE

353. VEE INRCNFGG ZG LVGFW HIRA V
HAZOFNGVE ZAAVYF WFGZNF RA YJF
IVNY RS FOFNM RNCVAZGU YR EZOF
LFMRAW ZYG ZATRUF.
—GVUHFE LHYEFN

354. QZS VHQWKWMQ HIVNEJWKM DS
EWOS WX QZS CSMQ VG JEE
HVMMWCES DVIEUM JXU QZS
HSMMWKWMQ GSJIM QZWM WM QIRS.
—AJKSM NJCSEE

82

355. PBTSA, T DIZO XZN'KP FTIUTIU
LIB XZN DIZO XZN'KP FTIUTIU, GNS SAP
IPTUAGZKF CTUAS SATID T'C
SZKSNKTIU XZN.   —LKWATP GNIDPK

356. WBQLQ VLQ WBLQQ WBTEUG T
VDOVKG AZLUQW. EVRQG, AVPQG,
VEM—WBQ WBTLM T PVE'W LQRQRXQL.
                        —TWVDZ GHQHZ

357. UYYUTXJQVXVLB ITL JBJIZZO
MVBHJVBLM IB PITM GUTD, BU AUBX
YLUYZL MUQ'X TLSUHQVEL XPLA.
                        —IQQ ZIQMLTB

358. FH QBL SDDJ OFLNIYDXDO
DCMDXFVDJHBPPE HQBH EIK NBJ OXBZ
PBKTQHDX RXIV BJ BKOFDJND
BJEZQDXD FJ HQD ZIXPO, IR BJE NPBLL
IX XBND, LFVMPE SE ZBPUFJT IJHI B
LHBTD BJO KHHDXFJT HQD ZIXOL "F BV
B VBXXFDO VBJ."
                        —HDO UBYBJBTQ

359. ZI Z QZXB ZC, Z GFH ZC'G PZVB.
ZI Z LTV'C, Z GFH ZC'G F IFXB.

—UFSQT UZNFGGT

360. D RTBBDHF CYH FWZH AKB
SHCCHB KB GKBXH SWC PKC AKB
NWPJY. —FWJYHXX KA GDPFXKB

361. B EBOOZQA JNSKUQ BOQ RQUU
VSZPQA RDQT WNPD KBOPTQOV
SVSBUUG MQQU PDQ TQQA MNO B
LSBOOQU BP PDQ VBEQ PZEQ.

—XQBT ONVPBTA

362. WTS RWSMT'A ZJBS AW HSA
JTUVZSYS GT J EJYYGJHS. GA'M TWA
J QOIPGK KWTBSUJTKS.

—GYGM EOYRWKZ

363. SUEEODS VOIBAXUV MGCE
WUXYGCU NBG VBD'E HBIU Y FYD OC
YHFBCE YC COHHN YC SUEEODS
FYAAOUV MGCE WUXYGCU NBG VB.

—PCY PCY SYWBA

84

364. ESMH KVW'PM ULPVUI, KVW'PM U
CAUAMCYUH; ESMH KVW'PM UA SVYM,
KVW'PM FWCA U GVXDADQDUH.

—SUPVXI YUQYDXXUH

365. YSJJHSBP HE S FDXAPJQOI
HXRPXKHDX, GOK KWPX SBSHX ED HE S
GHMNMIP JPVSHJ CHK.

—GHIIN MDXXDIIN

366. XPTVLYZYQ WJY QKZFYJYS VQ
LWOY ABYE UYA TPOA.

—OXVDY ZVTTVUWQ

367. S FE EFZOIACGY IAG EIEGAX FAC
EFZNVTACGY XLG AGDX.

—LFYIVC EFZESVVFA

368. CP JYXSX'U B NDSUX CVURIJ, C
ODV'J WVDN CJ. C YBGX ERUJ MXXV
JDIO MK AK PSCXVO QIBOKU JYBJ
UYX'O JSRUJ YXS YRUMBVO JD UZXVO
BV XGXVCVQ BIDVX NCJY AX.

—ABSEDSCX ZSDDZU

369. BAX ARSYXNB BRNG CL R QCSI'N
ICUX CN BM WSMFX BM R JRL BARB ACN
CLBXLBCMLN RSX NXSCMDN.

—AXIXL SMHIRLY

370. T ZIRIV IRIZ JIKTIRIN TZ
NTRPVHI FZLTK DSLIV T OPL GDVVTIN.

—NTDZI SPVN

371. IPJ QIPJU BNVPI N MGNO IQ YH
SNEJ, UWIP: "OQ HQW EJJT IPGI IPJ
MJL GBO JLKNIJYJBI PGM VQBJ QWI
QE QWU YGUUNGVJ?" UWIP MGNO: "N'TT
ONMKWMM NI SNIP HQW OWUNBV IPJ
BJLI KQYYJUKNGT."

—YNTIQB FJUTJ

372. R'V WNENA PXRWP CX KN OJVXDB...
R MXW'C MX JWHCQRWP.
WXC XWN BRWPUN CQRWP. R DBNM CX
KRCN VH WJRUB, KDC R MXW'C NENW
MX CQJC JWH VXAN.

—MXAXCQH YJATNA

373. DBJI WBCFLIGP TDD NOZCMP
IVWIEN EBJIGNU TCQ T NBBNOTWOI.

—ATI RIPN

374. PIR NFZ UP DR FDQR UP BPHIU,
GM PIQC ZP UNFU FU MGMUC PIR
SPRZI'U XFYYC F OGYQ PM UKRIUC.

—XFAGX OPYVC

375. GUU IRHOGZI? GU PNBB QZGP
IUOG; QN'BB ERCN GPN FZIGHDN
RYVQRV.   —OREHNB WUBTQVY

376. G OVT'U UIGTX AVHHGTH GW
IDYSUIR, DWEDJGYSSR PVLTGTH
AVHHGTH. GK PVLTGTH AVHHDLW
XTDB IVB UDPEUGTH UIDR SVVXDO UV
PVLTGTH PVUVLGWUW, UIDR BVQSO
WUYR IVPD YTO OV WGU-QEW.

—LGUY LQOTDL

377. U CYDYH KPOYR P ZPC YCSXNK
OS NUDY KUZ KUB RUPZSCRB JPMQ.

—GBP GBP NPJSH

378. ZDVEV HEV ZIA XNLMG AS
QEWNGVG—YOVHGWEV HLM INZD
QDNOMEVL.   —JVAEJV CWELG

379. W'AN VQTG MTNZX CWXP XPN
SNQ W'AN JNNQ SLYYWNF XV. PVC SLQG
CVSNQ HLQ SLUN XPLX HTLWS?
                  —NTWILJNXP XLGTVY

380. RCQH STUQGT QH UTSRPQFEK
HQEEK. QR HPKH RW HTGPSPRT RJW
TYYH, MIR QR AWTHF'R HPK CWJ BPS
RW HTGPSPRT RCTX.   —YSPUQT PEETF

381. K'JZ GZZS PDKSA FZA FKYLB
YWKLIYTFFH YDV WGDTL YKYLZZS
HZWVB, WSP LIZ DSFH LIKSA LIWL IWB
ADLLZS LIKSSZV KB LIZ RWVNZL
UIZVZ K IWJZ GZZS PDKSA LIZ FZA
FKYLB.   —VKLW VTPSZV

382. PKFSOU QIT SYL BFKOKCBYT FB.
JY DAQFPAD CD JXB X SQHCY XZQFD
F.B. BYLXDQKB.   —JYLTYII DKQPTQL

383. O GMCF TQZYJGQ OL'G VMYL
WOGLOAKJOGMQG JG INCB LMQ NQGL
CI LMQ YAOBYS DOAKWCB.

          —"BNG. SCZDMCNA,"
          MCQGL YAW NQOAQN

384. R YJBW LYSWW IWLH JL YVEW
GYRPY JTHGWS LV LYW HJEW IOSIVHW
JH J YOHMJTK: R YJBW J KVX GYRPY
XSVGQH WBWSA EVSTRTX, J IJSSVL
GYRPY HGWJSH JQQ JNLWSTVVT, JTK
J PJL LYJL PVEWH YVEW QJLW JL
TRXYL.   —EJSRW PVSWQQR

385. VONRSXN HCS QYVTZK CEK
TVMZZM EO BCZ CVOXK SP BZZOVAZMK
CVK BS ZOGSN YEFEOA SO BCZ ZXAZ!

          —"PDOIN HEOIZMRZVO," RVBEDI

386. MUQ'GP RPNCH UY JUZCNHP
ORDCDWUGXBM? ... ERDWB UY RDZ NX
TUXPY XENVDW IDER N IRUUAPP
JQXRDUW.   —TDZ TURWXUW

387. LAX EIQURZXIFLRQG QZ TFPPFNX
XPLFHURPATXGLP RG UQGSQG RG LAX
UFPL ZXM JXFIP FEEXFIP LQ
RGSRWFLX F SIFTFLRW RGWIXFPX RG
TDPWDUFI SRPQISXIP FTQGNPL LAX
TFUX EQEDUFLRQG.   —FGQGJTQDP
        XGORIQGTXGLFU AXFULA QZZRWXI

388. FTSPVQFA ONXKFAMX FPS UOS
KSXU VA UOS ICPZM; AC CUOSP
ONXKFAMX FPS XC WSASPCNX UC
UOSVP IVLSX, CP QFA KS XC SFXVZH
MVLCPQSM.   —SZVACP WZHA

389. IYNLUQ NZ M UMVQ WOMW
ZQXMYMWQZ WOQ VQA SYPV WOQ
IPJZ. NW MCZP ZQXMYMWQZ OGZIMALZ
MAL KNTQZ.   —UQPYUQ IGYAZ

390. B LVWSUI WT TKZSKUS RKJ IKU'E
XBMS EK EBYQ EK BURZKVS KUDS EXS
LKKI WT KU EXS EBNYS.
                    —TBNVWUB ZBEEXSCT

391. WZP YIAP FPO, IF I FPO, CRPF
KRW MKSQPXFIAAL IGGPIA WR YP. S
TSKC WZP YPK WRCIL APFF YIKAL; NMW
I ERYIK RT YL IBP SF KRW SK I
GRFSWSRK WR VKRE POIJWAL ZRE
YIKAL WZPL IXP.

　　　　　　　　　—VIWZIXSKP ZPGNMXK

392. TOLUKCKSF YV PISG WYEL
CNHWLVSLKSL, LBSLTM YM'V PHOL
MYOYKU CKN FHI NHK'M ULM MH WLCDL
GHPL QGLK YM'V HDLO.

　　　　　　　　　—SCMGF SOYPPYKV

393. C FIPY UFF GS WBCFXLYH, VON
MIGY IZ NBYG C XIH'N FCEY.

　　　　　　　　　—FCFCUH WULNYL

394. TX MCWD KAUWLUL LFJU GTGR'D
JWIU FDCUEL JTLUEWZAU, NFQ
MFQAGR'D CWPU DCU MFEAG GTPTGUG
TRDF LJFITRH WRG RF LJFITRH.

　　　　　　　　　—HUFEHU ZQERL

395. WG DIY NS'YS SUXASY ZGUJZ XG
ZSX I BGZ GY AIPS I VAUOB. NS
AIPSJ'X RFUXS BSVUBSB UD NS NIJX
XG YFUJ GFY VIYMSX GY YFUJ GFY
OUPSW.   —YUXI YFBJSY

396. NOG NOG SGMXV SXE IGVVUAQ
GO G XZA-XHH GZQ UE RGO OX
OKPPAOOHKC OBA EKVZAQ UE UZEX G
OAVUAO.   —MXM BXDA

397. LM FXL AZM ZXJ AGKJDYKI AEDZ X
JKYW-XICSJDELN RXGI DXTYK RXL
KHKG OSEDK TK DZK FXL ZK MLRK AXJ.
                    —CXFKJ DZSGTKG

398. HYCF ZMB AYHB KDFSZGCF—
IKBT'MB NYGB ZF AEGU ZF IKBT'MB
FEOBEGB BAFB'F. —OZMFKZ RZMNYBAC

399. DQ TCSJN-QDQI NIMSZ KI
MQZHISIE CQI BSMNIS MQE JKDZ DZ
DJ?   —MSVKDI XWQGIS

92

400. Q EQKB EQRB Z STFR, ZESTLI. Z
STFR UQIC HBP EQGL, LCTHI PHBLLBL
ZFP NQY CZQH.   —IQFZ IVHFBH

Clue One

This section offers a single clue, or letter equivalent, for each puzzle. If Z = A in cryptogram number one, then Z will equal A throughout that puzzle. Since each puzzle has its own code, the clue and letter equivalents will be different in each cryptogram.

1. O = C	28. X = I	55. W = S	82. O = Q	109. Z = P
2. S = T	29. R = V	56. S = M	83. G = Y	110. X = R
3. V = D	30. Z = W	57. Z = M	84. B = K	111. E = C
4. D = M	31. L = V	58. Y = N	85. B = T	112. X = R
5. O = C	32. Q = G	59. N = C	86. F = G	113. Q = G
6. G = H	33. W = B	60. R = L	87. C = B	114. C = M
7. A = C	34. X = C	61. P = B	88. A = V	115. S = H
8. J = S	35. L = Y	62. O = K	89. Y = L	116. Z = W
9. R = G	36. F = P	63. L = O	90. I = B	117. J = H
10. F = M	37. S = C	64. O = X	91. L = W	118. O = H
11. O = G	38. M = C	65. G = B	92. D = S	119. B = L
12. B = F	39. K = R	66. V = G	93. Q = M	120. R = M
13. B = M	40. M = P	67. Z = P	94. A = K	121. Z = F
14. W = B	41. G = T	68. Q = D	95. O = P	122. E = B
15. T = B	42. A = D	69. H = G	96. X = P	123. O = T
16. W = G	43. C = H	70. Q = P	97. L = V	124. N = C
17. P = V	44. D = Y	71. C = O	98. Z = F	125. H = M
18. L = P	45. M = J	72. K = B	99. J = C	126. A = C
19. X = K	46. Z = M	73. U = H	100. B = P	127. I = C
20. U = M	47. N = W	74. P = D	101. A = P	128. L = B
21. C = B	48. W = D	75. O = J	102. W = Y	129. H = B
22. A = Y	49. P = Y	76. B = C	103. F = L	130. M = L
23. B = M	50. G = F	77. B = P	104. X = W	131. H = B
24. H = K	51. D = W	78. C = T	105. E = B	132. V = B
25. Z = B	52. D = T	79. G = W	106. N = Y	133. F = L
26. H = M	53. K = D	80. Z = F	107. I = C	134. U = C
27. E = K	54. Y = F	81. N = F	108. Y = F	135. R = F

136. W = P
137. Y =N
138. Z = Y
139. X = C
140. M= F
141. P = B
142. M= B
143. A = J
144. O=Q
145. S = F
146. Q= C
147. C = L
148. D = M
149. N = M
150. V = U
151. U = B
152. P = V
153. A = B
154. R = T
155. B = M
156. V = F
157. M = A
158. S = C
159. B = K
160. F = G
161. T = F
162. D = P
163. C = W
164. W = Y
165. N = C
166. T = P
167. I = T
168. Y = M
169. A = B
170. P = M
171. W = M
172. D = J
173. I = L
174. J = F
175. M = F
176. B =M

177. A = B
178. N = G
179. S = P
180. H = C
181. Z= P
182. Z= B
183. L =W
184. N= Y
185. B = K
186. Z= B
187. C = G
188. G = L
189. N = V
190. U = M
191. T = G
192. H = F
193. P = F
194. M = F
195. V = B
196. P = F
197. Q = W
198. C = M
199. K = M
200. L = O
201. I = D
202. E = N
203. W = F
204. A = W
205. J = O
206. R = Y
207. W = M
208. B = Y
209. W = F
210. J = N
211. D = M
212. P = F
213. R = V
214. Y = L
215. P =W
216. J = P
217. I = B

218. Y = M
219. D = F
220. K = J
221. O= V
222. V = B
223. V = B
224. S = F
225. V = B
226. B =O
227. V = B
228. C = G
229. C = L
230. T = C
231. L = C
232. M = B
233. U = W
234. J = U
235. A = D
236. B = C
237. U = B
238. A = B
239. I = X
240. I = N
241. K = B
242. V = Y
243. E = H
244. W = G
245. Q = M
246. C = U
247. A = B
248. T = F
249. I = M
250. Y = L
251. T = C
252. P = H
253. D = L
254. M = G
255. J = F
256. I = T
257. G = R
258. X = L

259. T = R
260. Y = M
261. D = L
262. R = B
263. B = L
264. G = B
265. Y =M
266. E = P
267. S = X
268. P = C
269. R = B
270. Q= Y
271. G = M
272. P = D
273. Z = U
274. K = W
275. Z = W
276. L = K
277. Y = L
278. U = W
279. M = E
280. N = M
281. Z = V
282. U = L
283. G = S
284. O = V
285. O = P
286. E = Q
287. T = K
288. C = J
289. W = M
290. D = N
291. J = C
292. V = G
293. C = M
294. U = X
295. Q = F
296. F = B
297 S = F
298. G = F
299. B = P

300. Y = P
301. H= B
302. P = D
303. P = J
304. D= P
305. D = C
306. Q= B
307. F =H
308. S =N
309. D= C
310. N= C
311. M= L
312. Y = F
313. H=M
314. E = S
315. P = C
316. Z= L
317. U = V
318. W = B
319. T = L
320. H = M
321. E = F
322. A = B
323. G = C
324. U= M
325. G = W
326. V = D
327. H = V
328. R = J
329. Q= B
330. V =W
331. T = G
332. E = P
333. Z=M
334. S = F
335. E = M
336. E = L
337. L =W
338. D= L
339. L = C
340. B =D

341. M = C	353. L = B	365. N = Y	377. J = B	389. U = G
342. C = P	354. C = B	366. L = C	378. Q = C	390. N = B
343. B = C	355. U = G	367. Z = C	379. C = W	391. O = X
344. A = M	356. U = G	368. Z = P	380. G = P	392. T = P
345. I = M	357. H = G	369. G = K	381. R = C	393. W = C
346. D = Y	358. U = K	370. S = F	382. J = W	394. Z = B
347. L = K	359. N = C	371. L = X	383. D = K	395. R = Q
348. S = V	360. G = W	372. H = Y	384. I = P	396. P = C
349. C = P	361. O = R	373. F = Q	385. T = C	397. O = Q
350. D = K	362. K = C	374. D = B	386. O = Z	398. C = D
351. J = V	363. G = U	375. F = P	387. J = Y	399. T = F
352. E = V	364. L = B	376. E = P	388. W = G	400. E = L

Clue Two

This section offers a second clue, or letter equivalent for each puzzle. If M = T in cryptogram number one, then M will equal T throughout that puzzle. Since each puzzle has its own code, the clue and letter equivalents will be different for each cryptogram.

1. B = K	21. K = G	41. I = V	61. X = U	81. F = P
2. E = K	22. G = N	42. N = H	62. Q = B	82. E = P
3. H = P	23. Y = P	43. I = F	63. U = C	83. L = X
4. J = S	24. J = M	44. O = D	64. Q = Y	84. M = J
5. G = D	25. K = G	45. J = X	65. V = T	85. J = M
6. C = D	26. W = B	46. G = B	66. Z = B	86. J = M
7. W = Y	27. A = P	47. M = B	67. X = J	87. P = Y
8. G = M	28. V = G	48. E = F	68. Z = M	88. R = M
9. u = I	29. X = B	49. X = F	69. X = B	89. Q = G
10. Y = G	30. W = P	50. D = G	70. R = C	90. X = J
11. N = C	31. V = B	51. S = L	71. B = V	91. M = X
12. X = J	32. A = Q	52. Q = W	72. P = X	92. S = B
13. E = U	33. U = K	53. J = W	73. F = U	93. X = K
14. P= W	34. K = P	54. C = B	74. L =G	94. X = J
15. L = M	35. C = F	55. T = L	75. H = W	95. J = G
16. J = W	36. X = C	56. K = Y	76. L = V	96. F = G
17. B = K	37. T = D	57. H = F	77. M = K	97. A = B
18. A = U	38. F = X	58. J = P	78. H = V	98. G = K
19. N = G	39. A = H	59. G = P	79. R = C	99. B = G
20. S = P	40. O = V	60. Q= K	80. P = V	100. T = M

101. X = H	142. K = W	183. P = Z	224. O = B	265. D=W
102. A = C	143. K = Z	184. B = K	225. S = V	266. J = H
103. N = F	144. I = J	185. H= L	226. W = C	267. N = F
104. L = M	145. Q = Y	186. V = Z	227. S = D	268. Q = F
105. U = K	146. V = Y	187. A = F	228. O = B	269. B = K
106. B = W	147. K = J	188. Y = C	229. J = X	270. H= F
107. X = J	148. J = Z	189. Q = F	230. K = W	271. Y = W
108. X = R	149. F = B	190. R = G	231. N = B	272. Q = J
109. G = V	150. A = P	191. P = B	232. O = Z	273. R = J
110. Z = U	151. D = L	192. Y = Q	233. I = V	274. C =Z
111. Q = D	152. B = K	193. V = D	234. V = K	275. I = P
112. L = D	153. X = J	194. Q = C	235. B = C	276. V = D
113. X = M	154. D = V	195. D = K	236. Q = P	277. T = B
114. P = K	155. R = W	196. Y = P	237. M = D	278. N = M
115. P = B	156. F = P	197. T = C	238. Q = M	279. N = W
116. K = F	157. X = J	198. E = P	239. S = D	280. L = B
117. B = G	158. T = V	199. T = B	240. X = C	281. B = K
118. P = V	159. R = Z	200. V = H	241. A = K	282. H = D
119. X = M	160. V = K	201. B = M	242. I = F	283. A= N
120. O = C	161. Q = C	202. Q = L	243. L = B	284. K = F
121. C = K	162. H = K	203. V = P	244. F = C	285. G = B
122. T = P	163. K = V	204. U = Y	245. M = C	286. B = M
123. D = V	164. X = B	205. X = P	246. Z = K	287. Q= R
124. I = P	165. K = R	206. X = B	247. M = Y	288. E = K
125. O = B	166. B = V	207. M = T	248. O = V	289. G = J
126. C = G	167. T = B	208. N = K	249. E = B	290. E = F
127. R = B	168. O = W	209. O = M	250. I = W	291. Y = K
128. S = M	169. H = P	210. M = P	251. Q = F	292. Q = P
129 J = R	170. H = P	211. P = L	252. Z = M	293. D = P
130. T = V	171. K = V	212. G = W	253. X = B	294. C = L
131. T = L	172. Y = G	213. B = Q	254. Q = Z	295. T= M
132. I = W	173. C = P	214. N= P	255. H = D	296. Z = P
133. T = W	174. U = C	215. D = P	256. B = M	297. C = B
134. X = P	175. O = W	216. F = B	257. Z = N	298. V = K
135. Q = W	176. X = V	217. Z = M	258. N = B	299. V = L
136. L = B	177. Q = Z	218. R = L	259. L = J	300. F = N
137. I = B	178. X = C	219. M = K	260. X = H	301. S = M
138. T = C	179. V = X	220. D = C	261. T = D	302. D = M
139. V = G	180. J = W	221. C = P	262. Z = P	303. D = W
140. B = V	181. E = X	222. L = G	263. O = C	304. M = W
141. S = J	182. G = P	223. A = V	264. I = F	305. Q =H

306. F = R	325. M = V	344. I = V	363. C = S	382. P = G
307. H = C	326. K = V	345. O = B	364. X = L	383. K = G
308. P = B	327. D = C	346. Q = C	365. F = W	384. P = C
309. X = H	328. K = N	347. F = W	366. Z = M	385. R = B
310. Z = P	329. Z = J	348. N = K	367. E = M	386. T = J
311. W = G	330. O = X	349. T = M	368. G = V	387. T = M
312. E = M	331. L = C	350. R = B	369. H = W	388. L = V
313. X = J	332. T = N	351. T = P	370. R = V	389. I = B
314. K = B	333. A = Y	352. V = P	371. F = B	390. C = W
315. S = N	334. C = Z	353. I =P	372. Y = P	391. G = P
316. T = P	335. T = U	354. H = P	373. J = V	392. S = C
317. M = P	336. J = W	355. G = B	374. A = X	393. P = V
318. E = P	337. H = K	356. H = V	375 W = G	394. P - V
319. X = V	338. J = U	357. Y = P	376. A = J	395. V = C
320. W = B	339. I = V	358. N = C	377. N = G	396. M = B
321. L = C	340. D = C	359. U = P	378. W = U	397. T = B
322. D = K	341. I = U	360. J = C	379. I = Z	398. O = M
323. R = W	342 O = V	361. X = J	380. U = C	399. X = B
324. S = P	343. R = W	362. E = M	381. X = Y	400. H =R

Solutions

1. I've over-educated myself in all the things I shouldn't have known at all. —Noël Coward

2. A good listener is not someone who has nothing to say. A good listener is a good talker with a sore throat.
—Katherine Whitehorn

3. You can't teach an old dogma new tricks. —Dorothy Parker

4. You can say what you like about long dresses, butthey cover a multitude of shins. —Mae West

5. If you wantto get rid of stinking odors in the kitchen, stop cooking. —Erma Bombeck

6. Confusion is a word we have invented for an order which is not understood. —Henry Miller

7. Bathe twice a day to be really clean, once a day to be passably clean, once a week to avoid being a public menace.
—Anthony Burgess

8. There is no such thing as conversation. It is an illusion. There are intersecting monologues, that is all.　　　—Rebecca West

9. If you are foolish enough to be contented, don't show it, but grumble with the rest.　　　—Jerome K.Jerome

10. Believe me, you have to get up early if you want to get out of bed.　　　—Groucho Marx

11. Bigamy is having one husband too many. Monogamy is the same.　　　—Erica Jong

12. Juries scare me. I don't want to put my fate in the hands of twelve people who weren't even smart enough to get out of jury duty.　　　—Monica Piper

13. Early to rise and early to bed makes a male healthy and wealthy and dead.　　　—James Thurber

14. If a dog jumps onto your lap, it is because he is fond of you; but if a cat does the same thing, it is because your lap is warmer.
　　　—A.N. Whitehead

15. A memorandum is written not to inform the reader but to protect the writer.　　　—Dean Acheson

16. I don't make jokes—I just watch the government and report the facts.　　　—Will Rogers

17. My brother-in-law wrote an unusual murder story. The victim got killed by a man from another book.　　　—Robert Sylvester

18. A healthy male adult bore consumes each year one and a half times his own weight in other people's patience.　　　—John Updike

19. An intellectual is a man who doesn't know how to park a bike.　　　—Spiro T. Agnew

20. Getting married is a lot like getting into a tub of hot water. After you get used to it, it ain't so hot.　　　—Minnie Pearl

21. My grandmother was a very tough woman. She buried three husbands. Two of them were just napping.　　　—Rita Rudner

22. The Act of God designation on all insurance policies; which means, roughly, that you cannot be insured for the accidents that are most likely to happen to you.　　　—Alan Coren

23. If I had to give a definition of capitalism, I would say: the process whereby American girls turn into American women.
—Christopher Hampton

24. Physicians think they do a lot for a patient when they give his disease a name. —Immanuel Kant

25. Democracy substitutes election by the incompetent many for appointment by the corrupt few. —George Bernard Shaw

26. No man is responsible for his father. That is entirely his mother's affair. —Margaret Turnbull

27. Asking a working writer what he thinks about critics is like asking a lamp-post how it feels about dogs.
—Christopher Hampton

28. That youthful sparkle in his eyes is caused by his contact lenses, which he keeps highly polished. —Sheilah Graham

29. An expert is a man who has made all the mistakes which can be made in a very narrow field. —Niels Bohr

30. Health—what my friends are always drinking to before they fall down. —Phyllis Diller

31. I'm a wonderful housekeeper. Every time I get divorced, I keep the house. —Zsa Zsa Gabor

32. There are two classes in good society in England. The equestrian classes and the neurotic classes. —George Bernard Shaw

33. I don't buy temporary insanity as a murder defense. Breaking into someone's home and ironing all their clothes is temporary insanity. —Sue Kolinsky

34. I find the three major administrative problems on a campus are sex for the students, athletics for the alumni, and parking for the faculty. —Clark Kerr

35. Democracy means government by discussion, but it is only effective if you can stop people talking. —Clement Attlee

36. My sister has a social conscience now. She still wears her fur coat, but across the back she's embroidered a sampler that says "Rest in Peace." —Julia Willis

37. An appeaser is one who feeds a crocodile—hoping that it will eat him last.   —Winston Churchill

38. But I wasn't kissing her. I was whispering in her mouth.
                                                       —Chico Marx

39. In baiting a mousetrap with cheese, always leave room for the mouse.   —H.H. Munro

40. A diplomat these days is nothing but a headwaiter who's allowed to sit down occasionally.   —Peter Ustinov

41. There are times when parenthood seems nothing but feeding the mouth that bites you.   —Peter De Vries

42. Only good girls keep diaries. Bad girls don't have the time.
                                              —Tallulah Bankhead

43. Great restaurants are, of course, nothing but mouth-brothels. There is no point in going to them if one intends to keep one's belt buckled.   —Frederic Raphael

44. Eternity's a terrible thought. I mean, where's it going to end?
                                                   —Tom Stoppard

45. Well, I have one consolation. No candidate was ever elected ex-president by such a large majority!   —William Howard Taft

46. A great many people have come up to me and asked how I manage to get so much work done and still keep looking so dissipated.   —Robert Benchley

47. There are only two emotions in a plane: boredom and terror.
                                                   —Orson Welles

48. The hardest years in life are those between ten and seventy.
                                                    —Helen Hayes

49. I entertained on a cruising trip that was so much fun that I had to sink my yacht to make my guests go home
                                           —F. Scott Fitzgerald

50. Fish die belly-upward and rise to the surface; it is their way of falling.   —André Gide

51. I'm furious about the Women's Liberationists. They keep getting up on soapboxes and proclaiming that women are brighter

than men. That's true, but it should be kept very quiet or it ruins the whole racket. —Anita Loos

52. To eat well in England, you should have breakfast three times a day. —W. Somerset Maugham

53. I am ready to meet my Maker. Whether my Maker is prepared for the ordeal of meeting me is another matter. —Winston Churchill

54. A child develops individuality long before he develops taste. I have seen my kids straggle into the kitchen in the morning with outfits that need only one accessory: an empty gin bottle. —Erma Bombeck

55. Parents are the last people on earth who ought to have children. —Samuel Butler

56. What we want is a story that starts with an earthquake and works its way up to a climax. —Samuel Goldwyn

57. First need in the reform of hospital management? That's easy! The death of all dietitians, and the resurrection of a French chef. —Martin H. Fischer

58. The trouble with nude dancing is that not everything stops when the music stops. —Sir Robert Helpmann

59. I don't know how you feel about old age...but in my case, I didn't even see it coming. It hit me from the rear. —Phyllis Diller

60. I told my doctor I get very tired when I go on a diet, so he gave me pep pills. Know what happened? I ate faster. —Joe E. Lewis

61. The good thing about going to your twenty-fifth high school reunion is that you get to see all your old classmates. The bad thing is that they get to see you. —Anita Milner

62. A critic is a man who knows the way but can't drive the car. —Kenneth Tynan

63. I never travel without my diary. One should always have something sensational to read in the train. —Oscar Wilde

64. All creatures must learn to coexist. That's why the brown bear and the field mouse can share their lives and live in harmony. Of course, they can't mate or the mice would explode.
—Betty White

65. A man who has never gone to school may steal from a freight car, but if he has a university education, he may steal the whole railroad. —Franklin D. Roosevelt

66. Long experience has taught me that in England nobody goes to the theater unless he or she has bronchitis. —James Agate

67. Prison will not work until we start sending a better class of people there. —Laurence J. Peter

68. I wouldn't mind being called middle-aged if only I knew a few more one-hundred-year-old people. —Dean Martin

69. I was so long writing my review that I never got around to reading the book. —Groucho Marx

70. Many people consider the things which government does for them to be social progress, but they consider the things government does for others as socialism. —Earl Warren

71. The vote, I thought, means nothing to women. We should be armed. —Edna O'Brien

72. Whenever I feel like exercise, I lie down until the feeling passes. —Robert M. Hutchins

73. They used to shoot Shirley Temple through gauze. They ought to shoot me through linoleum. —Tallulah Bankhead

74. The Jews and Arabs should sit down and settle their differences like good Christians. —Samuel Goldwyn

75. No animal should ever jump up on the dining-room furniture unless absolutely certain that he can hold his own in the conversation. —Fran Lebowitz

76. Whoever said, "It's not whether you win or lose that counts," probably lost. —Martina Navratilova

77. I find it more satisfying to be a bad player at golf. The worse you play, the better you remember the occasional good shot.
—Nubar Gulbenkian

78. Moral indignation is in most cases two percent moral, forty-eight percent indignation, and fifty percent envy.

—Vittorio de Sica

79. There is nothing in the world I wouldn't do for Hope, and there is nothing he wouldn't do for me....We spend our lives doing nothing for each other.   —Bing Crosby

80. For certain people, after fifty, litigation takes the place of sex.
—Gore Vidal

81. If you want to do a thing badly, you have to work at it as though you want to do it well.   —Peter Ustinov

82. There was no need to do any housework at all. After the first four years the dirt doesn't get any worse.   —Quentin Crisp

83. History teaches us that men and nations behave wisely once they have exhausted all other alternatives.   —Abba Eban

84. Horse sense is the good judgment which keeps horses from betting on people.   —W.C. Fields

85. I used to be Snow White...but I drifted.   —Mae West

86. I could dance with you till the cows come home. Better still, I'll dance with the cows and you come home.   —Groucho Marx

87. When I came back to Dublin, I was court-martialed in my absence and sentenced to death in my absence, so I said they could shoot me in my absence.   —Brendan Behan

88. I eat too many TV dinners. I've gotten to the point where every time I see aluminum foil I start to salivate. —Ellen Orchid

89. England and America are two countries separated by the same language.   —George Bernard Shaw

90. I do not care to speak ill of any man behind his back, but I believe the gentleman is an attorney.   —Samuel Johnson

91. Now that I think of it, I wish I had been a hell-raiser when I was thirty years old. I tried it when I was fifty, but I always got sleepy.   —Groucho Marx

92. I have spent a lot of time searching through the Bible for loopholes.   —W.C. Fields

93. Man is the only animal that learns by being hypocritical. He pretends to be polite and then, eventually, he becomes polite.

—Jean Kerr

94. I majored in nursing, but I had to drop it because I ran out of milk. —Judy Tenuta

95. A genius! For thirty-seven years I've practiced fourteen hours a day, and now they call me a genius! —Pablo Sarasate

96. I don't have a photograph, but you can have my footprints. They are upstairs in my socks. —Groucho Marx

97. If you're fifty years old, you've probably owned so many cars you can't even remember all of them in order.

—Andy Rooney

98. I recently became a Christian Scientist. It was the only health plan I could afford. —Betsy Salkind

99. I have come to regard the law courts not as a cathedral but rather as a casino. —Richard Ingrams

100. Please accept my resignation. I don't want to belong to any club that will accept me as a member. —Groucho Marx

101. One morning I shot an elephant in my pajamas. How he got into my pajamas I'll never know. —Groucho Marx

102. Apart from cheese and tulips, the main product of the country is *advocaat*, a drink made from lawyers. —Alan Coren

103. For the man of fifty, it is always third and long yardage, with a nearsighted quarterback. —Bill Cosby

104. The latest scientific studies show that *all* mice and rats have cancer. —Julia Willis

105. Mother always told me my day was coming, but I never realized that I'd end up being the shortest knight of the year.

—Sir Gordon Richards

106. A food is not necessarily essential just because your child hates it. —Katherine Whitehorn

107. There are only two things a child will share willingly—communicable diseases and his mother's age. —Dr. Benjamin Spock

108. I was street-smart—but unfortunately the street was Rodeo Drive.   —Carrie Fisher

109. Business is a bore. I use that section of the paper to line the cat box.   —Sue Grafton, "E" Is for Evidence

110. For extra fun, play with the color control until I turn green.
—David Letterman

111. I will undoubtedly have to seek what is happily known as gainful employment, which I am glad to say does not describe holding public office.   —Dean Acheson

112. The really frightening thing about middle age is the knowledge that you'll grow out of it.   —Doris Day

113. Remarriage is an excellent test of just how amicable your divorce was.   —Margo Kaufman

114. My Uncle Charlie showed me where milk comes from.But I still like it.   —"Dennis the Menace," Hank Ketcham

115. On my fiftieth birthday, two nice things happened: I didn't think once about Brooke Shields and I wasn't taken directly to intensive care.   —Ralph Schoenstein

116. Every man I meet wants to protect me. I can't figure out what from.   —Mae West

117. Blondes have the hottest kisses. Red-heads are fair-to-middling torrid, and brunettes are the frigidest of all. It's something to do with hormones, no doubt.   —Ronald Reagan

118. The difference between divorce and legal separation is that a legal separation gives a husband time to hide his money.
—Johnny Carson

119. I learned to walk as a baby, and I haven't had a lesson since.
—Marilyn Monroe

120. Sometimes when I look at my children I say to myself, "Lilian, you should have stayed a virgin."   —Lilian Carter

121. At fifty, you know that if everything did not turn out as you had planned, it is not the fault of your parents. There are market forces at work.   —Karen DeCrow

122. If you want a place in the sun, you've got to put up with a few blisters. —Abigail Van Buren

123. Everything else you grow out of, but you never recover from childhood. —Beryl Bainbridge

124. The basic characteristics of any good investigator are a plodding nature and infinite patience. Society has inadvertently been grooming women to this end for years.
—Sue Grafton, *"A" Is for Alibi*

125. Children have never been very good at listening to their elders, but they have never failed to imitate them.
—James Baldwin

126. The only thing worse than a reformed cigarette smoker is an early Christmas shopper. —Liz Scott

127. He must have had a magnificent build before his stomach went in for a career of its own. —Margaret Halsey

128. Age is something that doesn't matter, unless you area cheese. —Billie Burke

129. One of my friends told me she was in labor for thirty-six hours. I don't even want to do anything that feels good for thirty-six hours. —Rita Rudner

130. I'm the most liberated woman in the world. Any woman can be liberated if she wants to be. First, she has to convince her husband. —Martha Mitchell

131. If truth is beauty, how come no one has their hair done in a library? —Lily Tomlin

132. If we could sell our experiences for what they cost us, we'd be millionaires. —Abigail Van Buren

133. It takes a woman twenty years to make a man of her son, and another woman twenty minutes to make a fool of him.
—Helen Rowland

134. The major concrete achievement of the Women's Movement of the 1970's was the Dutch treat. —Nora Ephron

135. I want to tell you a terrific story about oral contraception. I asked this girl to sleep with me and she said no. —Woody Allen

136. There's no place ina P.I.'s life for impatience, fainthearted-ness, or sloppiness. I understand the same qualifications apply for housewives.   —Sue Grafton, *"B" Is for Burglar*

137. Don't takeup a man's time talking about the smartness of your children; he wants to talk to you about the smartness of his.   —E.W. Howe

138. No woman marries for money; they are all clever enough, before marrying a millionaire, to fall in love with him first.
—Cesare Pavese

139. It's hard for me to get used to these changing times. I can remember when the air was clean and the sex was dirty.
—George Burns

140. I had a Jewish delivery: they knock you out with the first pain; they wake you up when the hairdresser shows.
—Joan Rivers

141. If...you can't be a good example, then you'll just have to be a horrible warning.   —Catherine Aird

142. The old theory was "Marry an older man, because they're more mature." But the new theory is: "Men don't mature. Marry a younger one."   —Rita Rudner

143. I haven't known any open marriages, though quite a few have been ajar.   —Zsa Zsa Gabor

144. Beware of the man who praises women's liberation; he is about to quit his job.   —Erica Jong

145. It is difficult to see why lace should be so expensive. It is mostly holes.   —Mary Wilson Little

146. I would rather lie on the sofa than sweep beneath it.
—Shirley Conran

147. The way to hold a husband is to keep him a little jealous; the way to lose him is to keep him a little more jealous.
—H.L. Mencken

148. The Republican Party couldn't make up their minds wheth-er I'd be mistaken for a trollop or for the Queen of England. But silly as the request was, I stopped wearing purple.
—Elizabeth Taylor

149. Hubert Humphrey talks so fast that listening to him is like trying to read Playboy magazine with your wife turning the pages. —Barry Goldwater

150. The most popular labor-saving device today is still a husband with money. —Joey Adams

151. Weight-lifting apparatus are a curious phenomenon— machines invented to replicate the backbreaking manual labor the Industrial Revolution relieved us of.
—Sue Grafton, *"E" Is for Evidence*

152. Husbands think we should know where everything is—He asks me, "Roseanne, do we have any Cheetos left?" Like he can't go over to that sofa cushion and lift it himself. —Roseanne Barr

153. When I was in labor, the nurses would look at me and say, "Do you still think blondes have more fun?" —Joan Rivers

154. Statistics are like a bikini. What they reveal is suggestive, but what they conceal is vital. —Aaron Levenstein

155. I made some studies, and reality is the leading cause of stress amongst those in touch with it. —Jane Wagner

156. It is only possible to live happily ever after on a day-to-day basis. —Margaret Bonnano

157. There is so little difference between husbands you might as well keep the first. —Adela Rogers St. John

158. Many a man has fallen in love with a girl in a light so dim he would not have chosen a suit by it. —Maurice Chevalier

159. You never really know a man until you've divorced him.
—Zsa Zsa Gabor

160. Whenever I date a guy, I think, is this the man I want my children to spend their weekends with? —Rita Rudner

161. I hate doing laundry. I don't separate my colors from my whites. I put them together. I let them learn from their cultural differences. —Rita Rudner

162. It seems to me I spent my life in car pools, but you know, that's how I kept track of what was going on. —Barbara Bush

163. If you can't say anything good about someone, sit right here by me. —Alice Roosevelt Longworth

164. My husband and I have figured out a really good system about the housework: neither one of us does it.
—Dottie Archibald

165. Men can read maps better than women. 'Cause only the male mind could conceive of one inch equaling a hundred miles.
—Roseanne Arnold

166. Sometimes I wonder if men and women really suit each other. Perhaps they should live next door and just visit now and then. —Katharine Hepburn

167. Were women meant to do everything—work and have babies? —Candice Bergen

168. When you're an orthodox worrier, some days are worse than others. —Erma Bombeck

169. I called in sick today—but as soon as I hung up the phone, I felt a lot better. —Bunny Hoest and John Reiner

170. When I was a girl I only had two friends, and they were imaginary. And they would only play with each other.
—Rita Rudner

171. When my cats aren't happy, I'm not happy. Not because I care about their mood, but because I know they're just sitting there thinking up ways to get even. —Penny Ward Moser

172. I found a long gray hair on Kevin's jacket last night. If it's another woman's, I'll kill him. If it's mine, I'll kill myself.
—Neil Simon, *Only When I Laugh*

173. My father told me all about the birds and the bees, the liar— I went steady with a woodpecker till I was twenty-one.
—Bob Hope

174. Years ago we discovered the exact point, the dead center, of middle age. It occurs when you are too young to take up golf and too old to rush up to the net. —Franklin P. Adams

175. Don't marry a man to reform him—that's what reform schools are for. —Mae West

176. The first time you buy a house you see how pretty the paint is and buy it. The second time you look to see if the basement has termites. It's the same with men. —Lupe Velez

177. I figure you have the same chance of winning the lottery whether you play or not. —Fran Lebowitz

178. And how come when you mix flour and water together you get glue. And then you add eggs and sugar and you get cake. Where does the glue go? —Rita Rudner

179. If the income tax is the price you have to pay to keep the government on its feet, alimony is the price we have to pay for sweeping a woman off hers. —Groucho Marx

180. The cliché is true. Men like cars and women like clothes. I only like cars because they take me to clothes. —Rita Rudner

181. I don't believe man is woman's natural enemy. Perhaps his lawyer is. —Shana Alexander

182. You know, by the time you reach my age, you've made plenty of mistakes if you've lived your life properly. —Ronald Reagan

183. There'sa time when you have to explain to your children why they're born, and it's a marvelous thing if you know the reason by then. —Hazel Scott

184. Personally, I think if a woman hasn't met the right man by the time she's twenty-four, she may be lucky. —Deborah Kerr

185. I want a man who's kind and understanding. Is that too much to ask of a millionaire? —Zsa Zsa Gabor

186. I prefer the word "homemaker" because "housewife" always implies that there may be a wife someplace else. —Bella Abzug

187. I suppose when they reach a certain age some men are afraid to grow up. It seems the older the men get, the younger their new wives get. —Elizabeth Taylor

188. Any mother could perform the jobs of several air-traffic controllers with ease. —Lisa Alther

189. When he is late for dinner and I know he must be either having an affair or lying dead in the street, I always hope he's dead. —Judith Viorst

190. Do you think my mind is maturing late, or simply rotted early? —Ogden Nash

191. Guilt is the price we pay willingly for doing what we are going to do anyway. —Isabelle Holland

192. Despite my thirty years of research into the feminine soul, I have not yet been able to answer…the great question that has never been answered: what does a woman want? —Sigmund Freud

193. I'd marry again if I found a man who had fifteen million dollars and would sign over half of it to me before the marriage, and guarantee he'd be dead within the year. —Bette Davis

194. From birth to age eighteen a girl needs good parents. From eighteen to thirty-five she needs good looks. From thirty-five to fifty-five she needs a good personality. From fifty-five on, she needs good cash. —Sophie Tucker

195. No coach ever shoots baskets with his players. You just don't want them to ever know that you can't shoot. —Bobby Knight

196. When a man opens a car door for his wife, it's either a new car or a new wife. —Prince Philip

197. All the things I really like to do are either immoral, illegal, or fattening. —Alexander Woollcott

198. I love the "dumb blonde" image. I have nothing to live up to. —Pamela Denise Anderson

199. There is one thing I would break up over, and that is if she caught me with another woman. I won't stand for that. —Steve Martin

200. Women are repeatedly accused of taking things personally. I cannot see any other honest way of taking them. —Marya Mannes

201. Most of the time I don't have much fun. The rest of the time I don't have any fun at all. —Woody Allen

202. Large naked raw carrots are acceptable as food only to those who live in hutches eagerly awaiting Easter.

—Fran Lebowitz

203. Unfortunately, sometimes people don't hear you until you scream. —Stefanie Powers

204. One of the great wits of all time was the person who called them Easy Payments. —George Burns

205. The years between fifty and seventy are the hardest. You are always being asked to do things, and you are not yet decrepit enough to turn them down. —T.S. Eliot

206. My idea of superwoman is someone who scrubs her own floors. —Bette Midler

207. Matrimony is a process by which a grocer acquires an account the florist had. —Francis Rodman

208. The only time to believe any kind of rating is when it shows you at the top. —Bob Hope

209. Motherhood is the most emotional experience of one's life. One joins a kind of women's mafia. —Janet Suzman

210. Americans have been conditioned to respect newness, whatever it costs them. —John Updike

211. I refuse to admit that I'm more than fifty-two even if that does make my sons illegitimate. —Lady Astor

212. Never feel remorse for what you have thought about your wife; she has thought much worse things about you.

—Jean Rostand

213. A bachelor never quite gets over the idea that he is a thing of beauty and a boy forever. —Helen Rowland

214. People who live in glass houses should pull the blinds when removing their trousers. —Spike Milligan

215. No matter how happily a woman may be married, it always pleases her to discover that there is a nice man who wishes that she were not. —H.L. Mencken

216. I sold my memoirs of my love life to Parker Brothers and they are going to make a game out of it. —Woody Allen

217. It's not whether you win or lose—it's how you lay the blame. —Fran Lebowitz

218. I hate to spread rumors—but what else can one do with them? —Amanda Lear

219. One learns in life to keep silent and draw one's own confusions. —Cornelia Otis Skinner

220. I like Jay Leno, and as a matter of fact, he is very concerned about my health. In fact, he insisted that I jog through Central Park about midnight tonight. —Johnny Carson

221. I have no money. I don't even have a savings account because I don't know my mom's maiden name. —Paula Poundstone

222. A woman without a man is like a fish without a bicycle. —Gloria Steinem

223. Football has two of the worst features of American life: violence separated by committee meetings. —George Will

224. All I have to say about men and bathrooms is…they're not real specific. —Rita Rudner

225. There is nothing more depressing than to read the list of the most popular stolen vehicles of last year and not find your car listed. —Erma Bombeck

226. Happy is a man with a wife to tell him what to do and a secretary to do it. —Lord Mancroft

227. There are three things I've yet to do: opera, rodeo, and porno. —Bea Arthur

228. There are two reasons why I am successful in show business, and I am standing on both of them. —Betty Grable

229. Old-fashioned political candidate: one whose bar bills exceed his media advertising budget. —Wendell Trogdon

230. It was a woman who drove me to drink, and I never had the courtesy to thank her for it. —W.C. Fields

231. Rose-colored glasses are never made in bifocals. Nobody wants to read the small print in dreams. —Ann Landers

232. Absence does not make the heart grow fonder, but it sure heats up the blood. —Elizabeth Ashley

233. Now that I'm over sixty, I'm veering towards respectability. —Shelley Winters

234. If you are all wrapped up in yourself, you are overdressed. —Kate Halverson

235. It's a good thing that beauty is only skin deep or I'd be rotten to the core. —Phyllis Diller

236. I bank at a women's bank. It's closed three or four days a month due to cramps. —Judy Carter

237. A woman who can cope with the terrible twos can cope with anything. —Judith Clabes

238. A man in love is incomplete until he has married. Then he's finished. —Zsa Zsa Gabor

239. To me natural childbirth is backwards. Everyone takes drugs today except when they need them. —Rita Rudner

240. My true friends have always given me that supreme proof of devotion, a spontaneous aversion for the man I loved.

—Colette

241. A friend doesn't go on a diet because you are fat. A friend never defends a husband who gets his wife an electric skillet for her birthday. A friend will tell you she saw your old boyfriend— and he's a priest. —Erma Bombeck

242. On my twenty-first birthday my father said, "Son, here's a million dollars. Don't lose it." —Larry Niven

243. Ask your child what he wants for dinner only if he's buying. —Fran Lebowitz

244. The most dangerous word in the English language is estimate...because estimate basically means Chapter Eleven.

—Rita Rudner

245. A mother is neither cocky nor proud, because she knows the school principal may call at any minute to report that her child has just driven a motorcycle through the gymnasium.

—Mary Kay Blakely

246. No matter how cold it is outside, never go into a liquor store wearing a ski mask.   —"Farcus," Waisglass and Coulthart

247. The only reason I would take up jogging is so I could hear heavy breathing again.   —Erma Bombeck

248. Give me my golf clubs, fresh air, and a beautiful partner, and you can keep my golf clubs and the fresh air.   —Jack Benny

249. My old boyfriend used to say, "I read Playboy for the articles." I used to say, "Right, I go to shopping malls for the music."   —Rita Rudner

250. One reason I don't drink is that I want to know when I'm having a good time.   —Lady Astor

251. Love is a fire. But whether it is going to warm your hearth or burn down your house, you can never tell.   —Joan Crawford

252. Is there a cure for a broken heart? Only time can heal your broken heart, just as time can heal his broken arms and legs.
                    —Miss Piggy

253. An after-dinner speech should be like a lady's dress—long enough to cover the subject and short enough to be interesting.
                    —R.A. "Rab" Butler

254. Husbands are like fires. They go out when unattended.
                    —Zsa Zsa Gabor

255. If you want something done well, get a couple of old broads to do it.   —Bette Davis

256. There is no pleasure in having nothing to do; the fun is in having lots to do and not doing it.   —Mary Wilson Little

257. The thing women have got to learn is that nobody gives you power. You just take it.   —Roseanne Barr

258. When I go to the beauty parlour, I always use the emergency entrance. Sometimes I just go for an estimate.
                    —Phyllis Diller

259. You never realize how short a month is until you pay alimony.   —John Barrymore

260. A bachelor's virtue depends upon his alertness; a married man's depends upon his wife's.   —H.L. Mencken

261. I've always believed in the adage that the secret of eternal youth is arrested development.   —Alice Roosevelt Longworth

262. You don't get over hating to cook, any more than you get over having big feet.   —Peg Bracken

263. I absolutely refuse to reveal my age. What am I? A car?   —Cyndi Lauper

264. A diplomat is a man who always remembers a woman's birthday but never remembers her age.   —Robert Frost

265. I know the difference between a good man and a bad one, but I haven't decided which I like better.   —Mae West

266. My choice in life was either to be a piano player in a whorehouse or a politician. And to tell you the truth, there's hardly any difference.   —Harry S Truman

267. She was a lovely girl. Our courtship was fast and furious—I was fast and she was furious.   —Max Kauffmann

268. The lovely thing about being forty is that you can appreciate twenty-five-year-old men more.   —Colleen McCullough

269. I know a lot of people didn't expect our relationship to last—but we've just celebrated our two months' anniversary.   —Britt Ekland

270. I don't see much of Alfred any more since he got so interested in sex.   —Mrs. Alfred Kinsey

271. His mother should have thrown him away and kept the stork.   —Mae West

272. A child of one can be taught not to do certain things such as touch a hot stove, turn on the gas, pull lamps off their tables by their cords, or wake mommy before noon.   —Joan Rivers

273. No man is regular in his attendance at the House of Commons until he is married.   —Benjamin Disraeli

274. When a woman tells you her age, it's all right to look surprised, but don't scowl.   —Wilson Mizner

275. Women want men, careers, money, children, friends, luxury, comfort, independence, freedom, respect, love and a three-dollar panty hose that won't run.   —Phyllis Diller

276. If you love someone, set them free. If they come back, they're probably broke.   —Rhonda Dicksion

277. An actor's a guy who, if you ain't talking about him, ain't listening.   —Marlon Brando

278. Why should people go out and pay to see bad films when they can stay at home and see bad television for nothing?
                    —Samuel Goldwyn

279. It goes without saying that you should never have more children than you have car windows.   —Erma Bombeck

280. Now, as always, the most automated appliance in a household is the mother.   —Beverly Jones

281. I have my own chopsticks. They have my initials on top. And Velcro on the bottom.   —Rita Rudner

282. A professor is one who talks in someone else's sleep.
                    —W.H. Auden

283. The mark of a true crush...is that you fall in love first and grope for reasons afterward.   —Shana Alexander

284. Even when freshly washed and relieved of all obvious confections, children tend to be sticky.   —Fran Lebowitz

285. Marriage is an alliance entered into by a man who can't sleep with the window shut and a woman who can't sleep with the window open.   —George Bernard Shaw

286. If love is the answer, could you please rephrase the question?   —Lily Tomlin

287. The art of acting consists in keeping people from coughing.
                    —Ralph Richardson

288. Marrying a man is like buying something you've been admiring for a long time in a shop window. You may love it when you get it home, but it doesn't always go with everything else.
                    —Jean Kerr

289. Marriage is not just spiritual communion and passionate embraces; marriage is also three meals a day, sharing the workload and remembering to carry out the trash.
                    —Dr. Joyce Brothers

290. Woman serves as a looking-glass possessing the magic powers of reflecting the figure of man at twice its natural size
—Virginia Woolf

291. When you get past fifty, you have to decide whether to keep your face or your figure. I kept my face.   —Barbara Cartland

292. I want to have children while my parents are still young enough to take care of them.   —Rita Rudner

293. Not all women give most of their waking thoughts to pleasing men. Some are married.   —Emma Lee

294. Whenever you want to marry someone, go have lunch with his ex-wife.   —Shelley Winters

295. Setting a good example for your children takes all the fun out of middle age.   —William Feather

296. When you're bored with yourself, marry and be bored with someone else.   —David Pryce-Jones

297. Before I met my husband, I'd never fallen in love. ...I stepped in it a few times.   —Rita Rudner

298. The easiest way for your children to learn about money is for you not to have any.   —Katherine Whitehorn

299. The follies which a man regrets the most in his life are those which he didn't commit when he had the opportunity.
—Helen Rowland

300. I prefer to forget both pairs of glasses and pass my declining years saluting strange women and grandfather clocks.
—Ogden Nash

301. Brass bands are all very well in their place—outdoors and several miles away.   —Thomas Beecham

302. Money, it turned out, was exactly like sex; you thought of nothing else if you didn't have it, and thought of other things if you did.   —James Baldwin

303. Psychiatrist: He is always called a nerve specialist because it sounds better, but everyone knows he's a sort of janitor in a looney bin.   —P. G. Wodehouse

304. The physician can bury his mistakes, but the architect can only advise his client to plant vines.   —Frank Lloyd Wright

305. I have the potential to be incredibly organized. Unfortunately, my organization lacks consistency.   —Helen Nash

306. Faith is something that you believe that nobody in his right mind would believe.   —Archie Bunker

307. Psychoanalysis is spending forty dollars an hour to squeal on your mother.   —Mike Connolly

308. I will never be an old man. To me, old age is always fifteen years older than I am.   —Bernard Baruch

309. I smoke ten to fifteen cigars a day. At my age I have to hold on to something.   —George Burns

310. Growing old is like being increasingly penalized for a crime you haven't committed.   —Anthony Powell

311. Women prefer men who have something tender about them—especially the legal kind.   —Kay Ingram

312. You see, dear, it is not true that woman was made from man's rib; she was really made from his funny bone.
—J. M. Barrie

313. The marvelous thing about a joke with a double meaning is that it can only mean one thing.   —Ronnie Barker

314. Psychiatrist: A man who asks you a lot of expensive questions your wife asks you for nothing.   —Sam Bardell

315. Why does a woman work ten years to change a man's habits and then complain that he's not the man she married?
—Barbra Streisand

316. Can you remember when you didn't want to sleep? Isn't it inconceivable? I guess the definition of adulthood is that you want to sleep.   —Paula Poundstone

317. There is a vast difference between the savage and the civilized man, but it is never apparent to their wives until after breakfast.   —Helen Rowland

318. Behind every successful woman…is a substantial amount of coffee.   —Stephanie Piro

319. A lie is an abomination unto the Lord and a very present help in trouble. —Adlai Stevenson

320. It has been said that a bride's attitude towards her betrothed can be summed up in three words: Aisle. Altar. Hymn. —Frank Muir

321. I don't plan to grow old gracefully. I plan to have face-lifts till my ears meet. —Rita Rudner

322. You know it's hard to hear what a bearded man is saying. He can't speak above a whisker. —Herman J. Mankiewicz

323. To lose one parent, Mr. Worthing, may be regarded as a misfortune; to lose both looks like carelessness. —Oscar Wilde

324. Income tax: It has made more liars out of American people than golf. —Will Rogers

325. A verbal contract isn't worth the paper it's written on. —Samuel Goldwyn

326. Literature is mostly about having sex and not much about having children; life is the other way round. —David Lodge

327. If you live long enough, the venerability factor creeps in; you get accused of things you never did and praised for virtues you never had. —I. F. Stone

328. If people behaved in the way nations do, they would all be put in straitjackets. —Tennessee Williams

329. It is better to have loafed and lost than never to have loafed at all. —James Thurber

330. Only one man in a thousand is a leader of men—the other nine hundred ninety-nine follow women. —Groucho Marx

331. Life is a tragedy when seen in close-up, but a comedy in long-shot. —Charlie Chaplin

332. We sleep in separate rooms, we have dinner apart, we take separate vacations—we're doing everything we can to keep our marriage together. —Rodney Dangerfield

333. Some people ask the secret of our long marriage. We take time to go to a restaurant two times a week. A little candlelight

dinner, soft music and dancing. She goes Tuesdays, I go Fridays.
—Henny Youngman

334. I always say a girl must get married for love—and keep on getting married until she finds it.　　　—Zsa Zsa Gabor

335. A short neck denotes a good mind. …You see, the messages go quicker to the brain because they've shorter to go.
—Muriel Spark

336. Sunburn is very becoming—but only when it is even. One must be careful not to look like a mixed grill.　　—Noël Coward

337. I never knew what real happiness was until I got married. And by then it was too late.　　　　　—Max Kauffmann

338. If I had my life to live again, I'd make the same mistakes only sooner.　　　　　　　　—Tallulah Bankhead

339. I enjoy convalescence. It is the part that makes the illness worthwhile.　　　　　　　—George Bernard Shaw

340. I don't deserve this, but I have arthritis, and I don't deserve that either.　　　　　　　　　　—Jack Benny

341. I kissed my first girl and smoked my first cigarette on the same day. I haven't had time for tobacco since.
—Arturo Toscanini

342. Love is much nicer to be in than an automobile accident, a tight girdle, a higher tax bracket or a holding pattern over Philadelphia.　　　　　　　　　—Judith Viorst

343. Love will never be ideal until man recovers from the illusion that he can be just a little bit faithful or a little bit married.
—Helen Rowland

344. There are only about twenty murders a year in London and many not at all serious—some are just husbands killing their wives.　　　　　　—Commander G. H. Hatherill

345. They say you shouldn't say nothing about the dead unless it's good. He's dead. Good.　　　　　—Moms Mabley

346. It takes a good deal of physical courage to ride a horse. This, however, I have. I get it at about forty cents a flask, and take it as required.　　　　　　　—Stephen Leacock

347. And my parents finally realize that I'm kidnapped and they snap into action immediately: they rent out my room.

—Woody Allen

348. Even though a number of people have tried, no one has yet found a way to drink for a living.   —Jean Kerr

349. I can trust my husband not to fall asleep on a public platform, and he usually claps in the right places.

—Margaret Thatcher

350. I've decided that perhaps I'm bulimic and just keep forgetting to purge.   —Paula Poundstone

351. Everybody hates me because I'm so universally liked.

—Peter De Vries

352. This is a free country, madam. We have a right to share your privacy in a public place.   —Peter Ustinov

353. All progress is based upon a universal innate desire on the part of every organism to live beyond its income.

—Samuel Butler

354. The optimist proclaims we live in the best of all possible worlds and the pessimist fears this is true.   —James Cabell

355. Edith, I know you're singing and you know you're singing, but the neighbors might think I'm torturing you.

—Archie Bunker

356. There are three things I always forget. Names, faces, and— the third I can't remember.   —Italo Svevo

357. Opportunities are usually disguised as hard work, so most people don't recognize them.   —Ann Landers

358. It has been discovered experimentally that you can draw laughter from an audience anywhere in the world, of any class or race, simply by walking onto a stage and uttering the words "I am a married man."   —Ted Kavanagh

359. If I like it, I say it's mine. If I don't, I say it's a fake.

—Pablo Picasso

360. I married the Duke for better or worse but not for lunch.

—Duchess of Windsor

361. A married couple are well suited when both partners usually feel the need for a quarrel at the same time.   —Jean Rostand

362. One doesn't have to get anywhere in a marriage. It's not a public conveyance.   —Iris Murdoch

363. Getting divorced just because you don't love a man is almost as silly as getting married just because you do.
—Zsa Zsa Gabor

364. When you're abroad, you're a statesman; when you're at home, you're just a politician.   —Harold Macmillan

365. Marriage is a wonderful invention, but then again so is a bicycle repair kit.   —Billy Connolly

366. Policemen are numbered in case they get lost.
—Spike Milligan

367. I am MacWonder one moment and MacBlunder the next.
—Harold Macmillan

368. If there's a worse insult, I don't know it. I have just been told by my friend Gladys that she'd trust her husband to spend an evening alone with me.   —Marjorie Proops

369. The hardest task in a girl's life is to prove to a man that his intentions are serious.   —Helen Rowland

370. I never even believed in divorce until after I got married.
—Diane Ford

371. The other night I said to my wife, Ruth: "Do you feel that the sex and excitement has gone out of our marriage?" Ruth said: "I'll discuss it with you during the next commercial."
—Milton Berle

372. I'm never going to be famous…I don't do anything. Not one single thing. I used to bite my nails, but I don't even do that any more.   —Dorothy Parker

373. Love conquers all things except poverty and a toothache.
—Mae West

374. One has to be able to count, if only so that at fifty one doesn't marry a girl of twenty.   —Maxim Gorky

375. Too caustic? To hell with cost; we'll make the picture anyway. —Samuel Goldwyn

376. I don't think jogging is healthy, especially morning jogging. If morning joggers knew how tempting they looked to morning motorists, they would stay home and do sit-ups. —Rita Rudner

377. I never hated a man enough to give him his diamonds back. —Zsa Zsa Gabor

378. There are two kinds of cruises—pleasure and with children. —George Burns

379. I've only slept with the men I've been married to. How many women can make that claim? —Elizabeth Taylor

380. This recipe is certainly silly. It says to separate two eggs, but it doesn't say how far to separate them. —Gracie Allen

381. I've been doing leg lifts faithfully for about fifteen years, and the only thing that has gotten thinner is the carpet where I have been doing the leg lifts. —Rita Rudner

382. *Grumpy Old Men* surprised us. We thought it was a movie about U.S. senators. —Wendell Trogdon

383. I shop because it's what distinguishes us from the rest of the animal kingdom. —"Mrs. Lockhorn," Hoest and Reiner

384. I have three pets at home which answer to the same purpose as a husband: I have a dog which growls every morning, a parrot which swears all afternoon, and a cat that comes home late at night. —Marie Corelli

385. Anybody who places his career in the hands of teenagers has to enjoy living on the edge! —"Funky Winkerbean," Batiuk

386. You've heard of Comrade Zhirinovsky? ...Think of him as Josef Stalin with a whoopee cushion. —Jim Johnson

387. The proliferation of massage establishments in London in the last few years appears to indicate a dramatic increase in muscular disorders amongst the male population.
—Anonymous Environmental Health Officer

388. American husbands are the best in the world; no other husbands are so generous to their wives, or can be so easily divorced.   —Elinor Glyn

389. Bridge is a game that separates the men from the boys. It also separates husbands and wives.   —George Burns

390. A friend is someone you don't have to talk to anymore once the food is on the table.   —Sabrina Matthews

391. The male sex, as a sex, does not universally appeal to me. I find the men today less manly; but a woman of my age is not in a position to know exactly how manly they are.
                                    —Katharine Hepburn

392. Pregnancy is much like adolescence, except it's more tiring and you don't get to leave home when it's over.
                                    —Cathy Crimmins

393. I love all my children, but some of them I don't like.
                                    —Lilian Carter

394. If what pleases some didn't make others miserable, you wouldn't have the world divided into Smoking and No Smoking.   —George Burns

395. So far we're either going to get a dog or have a child. We haven't quite decided if we want to ruin our carpet or ruin our lives.   —Rita Rudner

396. Zsa Zsa Gabor got married as a one-off and it was so successful she turned it into a series.   —Bob Hope

397. No man who has wrestled with a self-adjusting card table can ever quite be the man he once was.   —James Thurber

398. Kids are like husbands—they're fine as long as they're someone else's.   —Marsha Warfield

399. In forty-nine years He answered one prayer and this is it?
                                    —Archie Bunker

400. I live like a monk, almost. A monk with red lips, short dresses and big hair.   —Tina Turner

Index